THE PHANTOM GRIZZLY

MOMENTS OF TERROR, YEARS OF FASCINATION, A LIFETIME OF ADVENTURE

STEPHEN F. STRINGHAM, PHD

HANGAR 1 PUBLISHING

BOOKS BY STEPHEN STRINGHAM

Beauty Within the Beast

Kinship With Bears in the Alaska Wilderness

Bear Viewing in Alaska

Alaska Magnum Bear Safety Manual

When Bears Whisper, Do You Listen?

Negotiating Close Encounters With Wild Bruins

Ghost Grizzlies and Other Rare Bruins:

The Art and Adventure of Knowing Wild Bears

The Phantom Grizzly

Nearly Breakfast for a Grizzly Bear

Treasures of the Golden Bear

Bear Viewing
Association

To watch, to wonder,
and to conserve.

DEDICATED TO

Lynn Rogers,
Chuck Jonkel,
John Craighead & Frank Craighead Jr.

Pioneers of Bear Biology

COLOR PHOTOS AND VIDEO

To see all images and video in color, go to the QR code at the end of each chapter. Open your smartphone's camera and point it at the square. Your phone will automatically detect the code and display a prompt. Tap the link that appears to view the content.

CONTENTS

FOREWORD

LYNN ROGERS, PHD

My friend Dr. Steve Stringham and I have worked with bears since the late 1960s—a time when bear research was in its infancy and black bears were still being eliminated as dangerous varmints. In the late 1970s, we met at a bear conference. Steve was a kindred spirit. We immediately began sharing thoughts and comparing findings, which we still do to this day.

Over the years, we discovered that a black bear's clacking teeth, quick lunges, fast charges, and sudden slaps to the ground are just blustery displays, not ferocious threats prefacing attack – although similar displays *do* occasionally precede attack by a grizzly bear. We accepted these behaviors by black bears as harmless expressions of anxiety and stress. By responding appropriately, we built trust and have been able to accompany numerous bears as they went about their lives ignoring watchers and revealing more about how they live minute by minute, as well as about their foraging and social behavior than ever before.

That should not have been a surprise to anyone. Jane Goodall and Dian Fossey had long used essentially the same methods to learn about chimpanzees and gorillas. Steve and I went on to experience the same trust and safety with many of Alaska's coastal grizzly bears. Even though mother grizzlies have a reputation for being the most dangerous of all bears, mothers which learned to trust people never threatened us. On the contrary, they calmly nursed their cubs next to us, using us as human shields against males who dared not come that close in Katmai National Park. Tens of thousands of other people have now shared similar experiences at Katmai, at nearby McNeil Falls, and at numerous other bear viewing sites.

Everything we saw was the opposite of what we had long been taught. What bears showed us was contrary to the many fear-based beliefs that still persist today. Particularly devastating to bears is the confused notion that those which lose their "natural fear of people" become more likely to attack and must be killed.

In fact, bears don't have a "natural" – i.e., instinctive fear of humans, as such. But bears do have natural fears of predators, against which they must defend themselves violently when they cannot escape. Most attacks on humans are attempts to defend themselves from *us*. They are not the result of too little fear, but of too much. Although fear of human predation can impel bears to avoid us by a wider margin, when a close encounter does occur, a defensive bear is more dangerous than a trusting bear. Even though a defensive black bear usually flees, sometimes it does not dare immediately turn its back on an enemy; so it first attacks, inflicting a few bites or swats before running off. Defensive grizzly bears also usually flee, but are more likely than black bears to seriously injure or kill someone perceived as a predator. Trying to keep bears afraid of human predation through hunting them aggravates defensiveness and increases risk of defensive attack – the primary cause of serious or fatal injury by grizzlies. According to Steve, every time he hears of someone being mauled by a defensive bear, he wonders whether the attack could have been prevented if the bear had previously learned to trust people as much as do bears at Katmai and McNeil.

By winning the trust of bears, Steve and I have been able to closely observe them through tens of thousands of close encounters without being attacked. As bears have lost fear of human predation, they have grown to ignore us and calmly go about their natural activities even with a researcher nearby recording those activities minute by minute, day and night. We found that the kinder and gentler our methods, the more the bears revealed about their lives.

When bears hang out around humans, it's usually not to interact with us, which they normally try to minimize. Rather, there are two other reasons for being near people: to avoid enemies that dare not come so close, or to exploit a food source near us. While near people, most bears go out of their way to avoid offending anyone, lest we shoo them away. If we don't force bears to pay attention to us, for instance by blocking their access to prized food, by bullying them, pestering them, or crowding close for photos, bears pay little more attention to humans than they do to ravens or seagulls. That's why people can usually safely view bears along a salmon stream or garbage dump where there is plenty of food they can exploit with little human interference. The same thing can happen where people purposefully feed bears, so long as the bears know that when food runs out at one feeding station, there will be more food at another nearby station or in the wilds (please don't feed bears without first contacting an expert and learning how to avoid having that endanger you, other people or bears).

According to Steve, it's when preferred food is scarce and people are seen as rivals for this food, that problems can arise even with a bear that trusts people. Bears tend to treat human rivals like they treat bear rivals. They sometimes try to scare people into letting them have free access to their food. People who comply are rarely injured. Nor does a bear normally injure anyone that it respects too much to bully – much as it wouldn't dare bully a higher ranking bear, lest that other bear retaliate violently.

According to Steve, this is the grain of truth in conventional thinking that bears become dangerous when they lose their fear of people. It's not losing fear of human predation, contrary to sport hunter lore, but losing fear of human retaliation, that can erode a bear's normal self-restraint so much that it succumbs to temptation.

Of course, that danger wouldn't exist if we adequately minimized temptations that lure bears into rivalry with us – temptations like accessible groceries, garbage, gardens, pet food, and other attractants. We should avoid and prevent situations where a bear's hunger for some prize would exceed its fear of retaliation by us.

Even if a hungry bear can be scared away, it's likely to come back, just as it would come back to a salmon stream after higher-ranking bears have finished feeding. If a bear isn't already sufficiently respectful toward people, trying to dominate it in a contest over food or some other prize could be risky. So can trying to bully a bear unnecessarily. Hence Steve's tactic of escalating respect gradually and gently. He advocates winning a bear's compliance with ever more challenging human demands until compliance is so habitual that it carries over even to rivalry over food.

Steve argues that the key to peaceful bear-human coexistence is a management strategy designed like a stool supported by four legs. (1) *Motives for aggression*: Avoid being perceived by bears as rivals for prized food, or as predators, or as prey. If bears associate people with sources of abundant food, over which there is no conflict, the association is seldom dangerous. But persistently famished bears can be dangerous, especially to people who impede a bear's attempts to obtain prized foods. [2] *Educate bears*: Let them live long enough to learn how to coexist with us. Teach them which locations they must avoid, as well as those where they are allowed so long as they comply with our demands – including how close they can come to us or to our homes. Teach them which behaviors are forbidden around us. (3) *Enhance trust*: Teach bears that they need not fear attack by us so long as they abide by our boundaries and limits. This can minimize risk of defensive attack. (4) *Maintain respect.* Teach bears that we will retaliate like higher ranking bears if they dare violate our boundaries or limits. Maintaining fear of retaliation can curb any tendency a bear might have to dominate humans or to prey on us.

As Steve often says, *"It isn't what you don't know that's a problem, it's what you know that isn't so."* People will not coexist with animals they fear, especially when that fear is greatly exaggerated. Although old fear-based beliefs die hard, we have to keep trying to publicize the truth about how to minimize risk and stress to both people and bears.

In this book, Steve recalls some of the kinds of experiences with black and grizzly bears that made us question our fears and want to learn more – which led to us discovering how ready most bears are to peacefully coexist with people, so long as we win their trust and avoid luring them into conflicts with us over food, in addition to maintaining their respect as if we were benign higher-ranking bears, not predators. I hope these stories have the same effect on you.

Bear safety and body language are only two facets of Steve's research. During the mid-1980s, the US Fish & Wildlife Service compiled all science on grizzlies into the **Grizzly Bear Compendium**. Most of the chapter on bear population dynamics was based on his research.

In addition to Steve's contributions as a scientist, he has applied his knowledge to real world challenges while working with the US Forest Service, US Fish & Wildlife Service, US Geological Survey, and Environmental Protection Agency; as Scientific Director of the Environmental Office of the Blackfeet Nation, as Director of the Bear Viewing Association, and as an independent ecological consultant through his company WildWatch. He led efforts that prevented construction of an ill-conceived 12-billion dollar pipeline through the heart of wildlife habitat in Vermont's Green Mountains. He later nearly lost his life exposing preparations by an organized crime syndicate for massive dumping of hazardous wastes on the Blackfeet Indian Reservation.

Steve also taught in the Blackfeet and Salish Kootenai Indian Nations, as well as at a number of universities, including the University of Alaska. He has taught field courses, and has guided thousands of wildlife viewers. Steve has given hundreds of public talks about bears and has published several books, with more on the way. His website, BearViewingAssociation.org, offers a wealth of additional information on bears. He has published more than 20 peer reviewed technical papers. His writings have reached over 100,000 readers on the Research Gate scientific website, in addition to readers on other venues. Research Gate rated interest in his research higher than 79% of all 17 million other scientists on the website, and higher than 80% of all other scientists studying animal communication.

PROLOGUE

My memory is a network of vivid details against a backdrop of foggy landscapes, of experiences that I recall with great clarity and those which had long been forgotten until triggered into vague recollection as I struggled to remember all that happened so long ago.

Perhaps clearest of all is the image of the Phantom Grizzly silhouetted against an autumn moon – a huge orange eye looking down at me from above Trapper Peak. Near where the pupil of the moon's eye would have been, was that of the grizzly, as its head was seen in silhouette, etched like an inlay of obsidian on an orb of glowing amber.

Beautiful. Terrifyingly, spellbindingly beautiful. Until the bear roared. Then glacial melt water seemed to cascade over me and sluice through every vessel in my body, eroding my strength, leaching my confidence, draining me of energy and every emotion except fear. Only will power kept me from falling to the ground, cowering and trembling, certain that death had come to claim me.

From fear are born awe, reverence, and worship. Small wonder that so many Native peoples prayed to this most humbling of Spirits. So too did I on many a night while grizzlies padded around me in the darkness. Yet no animal being has ever given me greater joy than some of those same bears

I

as they fished for salmon or nursed cubs or snoozed within a few yards of me during daytime.

Steve Stringham

1: A grizzly bear's head silhouetted against an autumn moon (illustration).

1

BEARANOIA & DISNEYESQUE

Since my birth in 1946, I've had nearly 20,000 close bear encounters. This book focuses on a handful of my earliest encounters in California and Montana, mainly during 1960-1969, involving numerous black bears and one grizzly. Even while earning my BSc degree in college, I knew little about bears except for conventional wisdom, much of which was (and is) distorted by bearanoia or Disneyesque. Only gradually did I get to know bears well enough to recognize those distortions and see past them to begin knowing bears as they really are – animals with a wide range of temperaments from friendly to homicidal, but generally preferring to live and let live with humans.

I suspect that you will enjoy the youthful exuberance and irreverence of a young scientist at the dawn of his career. Some of those early experiences were especially entertaining, dramatic and revealing – such as being stalked by the Phantom Grizzly one dark night, or, on another occasion, crawling into a den and coming eyeball to eyeball with a black bear.

My writings, photos, and video are as close as I can come to let other folks get a sense of what it is like to meet these magnificent animal beings up close and personal. The encounters described herein are typical bear-human interactions as I have experienced them, in stark contrast to the rare cases of extreme aggression which make up the bulk of mass media articles and of tales told at campfires or in bars.

If you start reading this book convinced that people can't be safe around bears that don't fear them – so-called habituated bears – fine. Don't take my word for anything. Believing follows seeing; so see for yourself. Skepticism is useful, so long as you keep an open mind and update your convictions to fit newly acquired facts and experiences, rather than acknowledging only those facts and experiences which fit preconceptions. By sharing some of my close encounters with you vicariously, I hope to help you see bears through my eyes, as well as through my science.

In addition to reading my books, you might follow embedded links to the websites of the Bear Viewing Association (BearViewingAssociation.com), Facebook (Bear Viewing Association), and YouTube (WildWatch2023) where you can see hundreds of additional photos as well as video clips. Better yet, join an excursion to watch bears first-hand, much as hundreds of thousands of other people have done. My insights on bear safety have been published in two books: *Alaska Magnum Bear Safety Manual* and *When Bears Whisper, Do You Listen*? A host of other insights on bear behavior and ecology have been published in peer-reviewed scientific journals.

Living and Dying With Bears

Bear attacks loom very large in our minds because they loom very large in our fears. Humans have likely feared bears for as long as humans and bears have been in contact.

In Europe, contact with bears began tens of thousands of years ago for our distant Cro-Magnon ancestors, and far earlier for our Neanderthal and Denisovian cousin species.

In fact, this fear likely began as soon as humans migrated from the interior of Africa to its northern coast, where they would have encountered brown bears. Once humans crossed the land bridge to the Mid-east roughly 200,000 years ago, then spread throughout Eurasia, they would have also encountered sun bears, sloth bears, Asiatic black bears, panda bears, brown bears and cave bears.

Both humans and brown/grizzly bears may have spread from Eurasia across the Bering Land Bridge onto this continent over 100,000 years ago. But the earliest surviving lineages of brown bears did not reach here until 70,000 years ago, eventually becoming well established as far east as the Mississippi River. This was achieved despite competition from endemic giant short-faced bears, which were up to twice as large as brown bears. Throughout the later cycles of the Pleistocene Ice Age, short-faced bears reigned supreme in North America, preying on mammoths, ground sloths, and other huge herbivores whose populations were supported by the highly nutritious Mammoth Steppe vegetation. However, as the Pleistocene came to an end, the warming climate gradually wiped out the Mammoth Steppe. As this food supply diminished, the enormous Pleistocene herbivores did too. Deprived of those prey, giant short-faced bears followed them into oblivion.

It was not until climate change debilitated giant short-faced bears and other Pleistocene megafauna, that permanent humans colonies were able to flourish in North America, roughly 14,000 yrs ago. Brown bears also benefited from the demise of short-faced bears. More commonly known as grizzlies in North America, brown bears reigned supreme during all the millennia that humans were armed mainly with spears, fire, dogs, poison, and eventually primitive fire arms. Only the invention and wide distribution of repeating rifles in the 1800s gave humans an overwhelming advantage over grizzlies. Although grizzly and black bears have continued to maim and kill people, it's far less common than we are led to believe.

Blood-Spattered Spectacles

Growing up, nearly everything I heard or read about bears emphasized their wanton savagery. I was thrilled by magazine stories and books about hunting bears or about someone being stalked and attacked. Bears were fearless, ferocious, and terrifying. Their speed was lightening fast. A bear's fangs were daggers and its claws were razor-sharp. Its eyes burned with fury. Saliva and blood drooled off its teeth. Its massive jaws could crush boulders. Bears were monsters. With no more dragons to slay, real men killed bears, proving their courage and gaining lifelong bragging rights for selflessly protecting the public. I wanted to do it too — until I began learning how vastly different those near-mythical monsters are from typical bears.

All too often, the media teach people to expect any bear to bully or attack anyone that it doesn't fear. Worse, the attacks which such media present are dramatized by being seen through proverbial blood-spattered spectacles which color grizzlies as raving demons whose only just fate would be a fearless hunter's bullet through the heart. Terror sells, especially to readers who relish imagining themselves as heroes saving fair damsels. Stories of innocent women being savaged by bears have an implicit sadomasochistic sexual element. Hence the terms predator porn, bear-porn, and Bjorn-porn. Bjorn is a Scandinavian word for bear.

* * *

Even if attack stories are not sensationalized, merely focusing on attacks or near- attacks, can bias readers to expect an attack by any bear. This is analogous to expecting any motor vehicle to crash. If the only thing you knew about cars and airplanes were that they maim or kill thousands of people each year, then you'd likely never want to ride in one. Certainly, it took me several days before I dared drive a car after being a passenger in one that was partly crushed by a logging truck. More than a year passed before I dared ride in a car driven by anyone else. Here on Alaska's Kenai Peninsula, where the Sterling Highway narrows down to two lanes between Tern Lake and Sterling, horrendous auto crashes are so common that I was in far greater danger driving to and from my study site near the confluence of the Kenai and Russian Rivers, than I was from bears at the site.

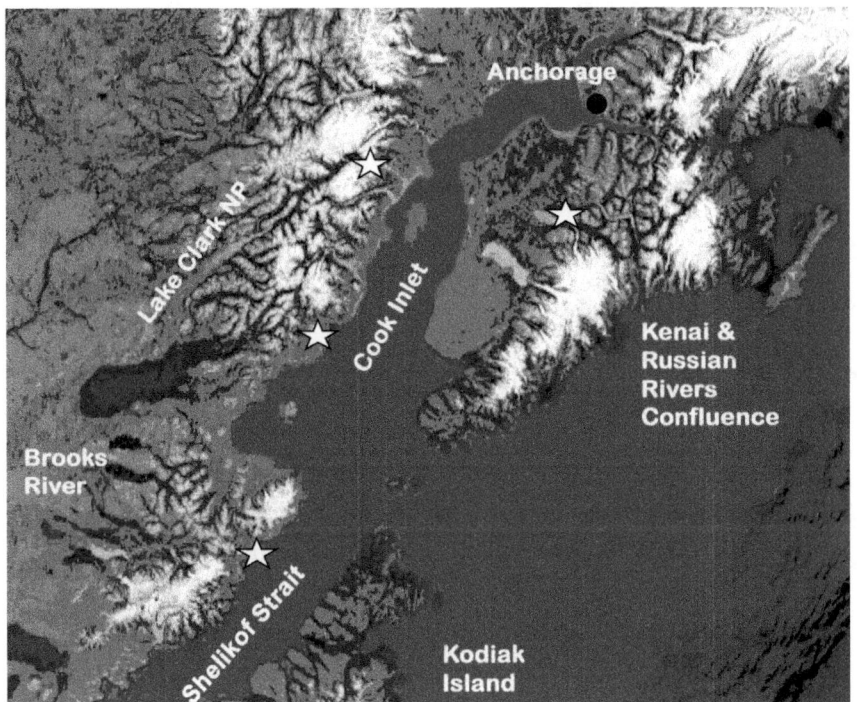

1.1: My main study areas in Alaska are marked with white stars: Diving Bear Cove (upper left), Chinitna Bay (center left), Katmai National Park (lower left), Kenai and Russian Rivers confluence (upper right) (Google Earth image).

Even more dangerous is flying in a small plane (1 – 10 passengers). Alaska's unpredictable winds, sudden fog banks, and other weather events make piloting so hazardous that I will ride in a plane only if the pilot is a professional with long experience. Even then, they are risky. On one flight home from the Alaska Peninsula, the dense fog suddenly filled the sky, forcing us to fly blind, except for GPS. That kept us from crashing into a mountain but didn't allow us to land. Not until the fuel was nearly down to fumes did a hole in the fog open up enough for us to see the runway and dive through to a gentle touchdown. At my Chinitna Bay study site, three planes with professional pilots crashed in a single day due to unusually poor landing conditions. A plane with six passengers and a professional pilot disappeared on their way to my study site in Katmai National Park. On 31

July 2020, a plane on its way to my Diving Bear Cove study site crashed, killing seven people. By contrast, during that same period, only two people have been killed by bears in these areas – Tim Treadwell and Amie Huguenard in 2003 at Katmai, due largely to Tim's refusal to follow standard safety precautions, even when an extreme food shortage made bears especially belligerent.

Despite the dangers of auto and airplane crashes, most people don't avoid those forms of transportation. Instead, they take precautions while traveling. Also, they know — both from statistics and from personal experience — that only a tiny fraction of rides end in tragedy. The same is true for coexistence with bears even here in Alaska where we have a tenth of North America's black bears and half its grizzly/brown bears.

When the media reports on so-called bear attacks, they are often not attacks at all, but rather a misunderstanding of bear behavior. Instances of a curious bear approaching people, or a frightened one trying to scare them into leaving it alone, can be blown out of proportion and paint the bear in an evil light. This was the case regarding two minor incidents involving a woman with the initials KR that were reported as attacks in a Montana newspaper:

- When wildlife were killed by vehicles in Yellowstone National Park during the early 1990s, carcasses were dumped at an out-of-the-way site where they were scavenged by bears. There were signs on the service road to the carcass dump warning people to avoid it. However, in 1994, KR and two friends bicycled there hoping to see bears. Stopping at the bottom of a steep hill, they spotted a sow grizzly with two cubs about forty feet away. KR reported that the sow jumped up and charged them, whereupon she and her companions turned and peddled away. However, contrary to the article, this could not have been an attack; for the sow could have covered the distance to KR in a couple of seconds, and been tearing into the gawkers before they could have begun to flee even if they were peddling down a steep hill rather than up one. Any "charge" by the sow was just a threat, an attempt to drive intruders away – much as when someone chases a bear or dog out of their yard. Threat-charges seldom end in attack, which is why they are misnamed bluff charges.

- Nor has injury resulted during any of the hundreds of times when I or someone I observed was approached by a walking bear – such as the one that KR encountered in Alaska's Denali National Park. While she was hiking and making plenty of noise to alert any nearby grizzly, a subadult appeared out of the willow shrubs thirty feet away. It approached within one or two arm's lengths of KR and began sniffing the air. When she waved her hands in front of its face, the subadult backed off slightly. When she started throwing rocks at it, the subadult left. Clearly, the only one attacked was the bear.

- A woman who attended one of my bear safety classes told of being chased down a road for a few hundred yards until a passing car picked her up. However, given that a bear can sprint at up to 45 ft/sec, it could have caught her in mere moments — long before she was "rescued" by the motorist — had that been the bear's intent.

- A man who attended another class told of being stalked by a bear. When I asked how he recognized that he was being stalked, and not just followed, he responded that stalking and following are the same thing. Not so! Stalking implies following sneakily with the intent to victimize the target person or animal. A stalking predator usually tries to remain undetected. It moves forward only when the victim won't notice, or it tries to remain hidden from its intended victim. The man in my audience had not actually been stalked, just followed – which is not diagnostic of intent to attack. There are other reasons why the bear might have been following him.

- Perhaps it was curious or just walking in the same direction on the same trail, as has happened to me on numerous occasions. In that event, I usually stepped off the trail to let the bear pass. Occasionally, a bear followed me off the trail to investigate me. But typically the bear just continued down the trail. In one case, the bears following me were a mother coastal grizzly with two cubs. They stayed at least thirty feet behind me for several hundred yards until I found a spot where I could climb off the trail, whereupon the sow and her brood sped up, passed me, and continued on, walking faster than I could have jogged. Far from stalking me, she had been politely holding her speed down to mine until I was finally considerate enough to let her pass. I had been like a slow driver in the fast lane. On the other hand, when the Phantom Grizzly followed me for a couple of hours on a dark night in Montana, I suspect that it was indeed sizing me up as prey – as detailed in Chapter 3.

Gross exaggeration also applies to many of the so-called attacks streaming on Youtube. Attacks are rare, so real footage is much more so. Most of the true attacks I've seen footage of were by a captive bear or, in two cases, by a wild sloth bear in India. In one of these cases, the man was not attacked until he knelt down beside an injured sloth bear to take a selfie with it.

This isn't of course to deny that some people really do get chased by a bear, much as some get chased by a dog. Some chasing dogs bite; so do some chasing bears. Some chases are domineering, intended to chastise the victim. Rarely, some chases are predatory, intended to capture and eat the victim. The motive for other chases isn't known, if only because the "victim" escaped unharmed, as allegedly happened to a bicyclist who claimed that he out-raced a grizzly that chased him. Actually, the video of that incident is demonstrably phony.

Escaping unharmed is a best-case scenario. In a worst case, the victim is seriously injured, permanently maimed, or killed. Since

1900, North American bears have killed roughly 200 people and injured another 800 or so. Fortunately, the numbers of attacks per decade and per million people on this continent quit increasing a few decades ago.

Exaggerating the number and severity of attacks, or focusing on them so exclusively that they seem far more typical than they really are, does nothing to make people safer. Quite the contrary. Excessive fear of bears – bearanoia – can cause overreactions that backfire, sometimes fatally. Shooting and merely wounding a grizzly, or fleeing in panic, could trigger attacks that wouldn't have otherwise occurred. At the other extreme, bearanoia sometimes causes people to harass or kill even innocent bears on the principle of *better safe than sorry*. Worse, a bullet that misses a bear might hit a human. I fear bears less than I fear gun-totting people who aren't skilled with firearm use during emergencies, or who shoot when a non-violent response could suffice.

Rose-Colored Glasses

1.2: Adult male grizzly with fresh claw wounds to his neck.

1.3: This male has scars on his forehead and muzzle, including one beside his right eye. Eye-side scars are so common that I wonder whether fighting males try to blind each other.

Bearanoia isn't the only impediment to peaceful bear-human coexistence. Another is denying the real challenges of coexistence. Of course, the very idea of living in peace with bears will strike some people as a far-fetched fantasy, spawned by reading children's novels like Walt Morey's classic tale *Gentle Ben* or watching too many Disneyesque movies and cartoons like *Brother Bear*. Mistaking such fiction for reality fosters expectations that people will be safe so long as they radiate serenity and love toward bears. All too often, risk deniers don't bother implementing essential precautions. Such neglect is epitomized by the late TV talk show guest and self-styled eco-samurai Tim Treadwell. In 2003, he and his lady Amie Huguenard ignored most safety measures when they camped near an Alaskan salmon stream where famished bears were trying to catch the few salmon available that year. Tim had no pepper spray and did not surround his camp with an electric fence. Worse, he harassed even dominant boars, according to notes in his journal written in the days before his death. I'd seen him do the same thing on other occasions, and wondered how he could imagine that adult males, which were covered with battle scars, (Figure 1:2 and Figure 1:3) and which tolerated no disrespect from their ursine subordinates, would tolerate disrespect from an obnoxious human smaller than a two-year-old cub? Their tolerance for Tim's antics amazed me then. I warned Tim that tolerance isn't limitless, but he dismissed my warnings. He saw even dominant males through proverbial rose-colored glasses — until he and Amie were killed and eaten by two of them.

Bear Safety Recommendations

When I began teaching my course *Bears and Bear Safety* through the University of Alaska, I recommended that my students read each of the existing manuals on bear safety. I informed students which advice in those manuals was still current and which had become obsolete due to recent discoveries by bear researchers, including myself. Eventually, to provide updated advice, and to fill gaps left by the other authors, I wrote a series of new textbooks.

- *Alaska Magnum Bear Safety Manual* covers ways to avoid having encounters, and basic methods of coping with typical encounters.
- *When Bears Whisper, Do You Listen?* covers advanced techniques to cope with typical encounter scenarios as well as atypical scenarios. This manual is tailored to folks who are so likely to encounter bears that they are willing to learn more about how to deal with encounters so as to avoid provoking aggression, or to pacify a bear that is already upset.
- *Ghost Grizzlies and Other Rare Bruins*: provides details for distinguishing the species, age and sex of a bear, as well as for distinguishing one bear from another.

STEPHEN F. STRINGHAM, PHD

Here are a few key tips from those books.

Avoiding Unwanted Encounters

- Unless you are preparing a meal or eating, try to avoid being near food that a bear could smell. Try to avoid any insect repellent or cosmetic that smells like food (e.g., citronella smells like ants; some shampoos have a fruity odor), or odors that might stimulate a bear's curiosity (petroleum products). Anything you carry that has a bear-attracting odor should be sealed to minimize the release of the odor. It should be packed in a bear-proof container so that if you have to surrender the container to a bear, the bear can't get the attractants inside.
- If you have reason to expect a bear on a trail, at a fishing site, or in any other area, you might want to avoid that area.
- If you can't or won't avoid an area likely to have a bear, make lots of noise as you approach. Bear bells seem useless for that purpose. Talking can help a little, but the sounds of voices are easily smothered by the sounds of wind or flowing water. Also, the sounds of talking can hide any sounds a bear might make, which could otherwise alert you to its presence and location. Although many folks yell "Hey bear!" with an abrupt harsh tone, some bears respond to that as a threat. They tend to react better to a more melodious, drawn-out "HHHeeellllooo once every few minutes." So that's what I use. I listen between yells on the chance I might hear a bear, perhaps huffing and snapping its jaws, or breaking branches as it approaches me or retreats. Hearing bears up ahead has helped me avoid several unwelcome close encounters.

Coping With Encounters

- If the bear doesn't know I'm nearby, I try to avoid revealing my presence when I detour around the bruin. (Bruin is an archaic term for bear).
- Most attacks are launched from within 50 yards of the victim; nearly all are launched from within 100 yards. So if I am over 100 yards away, chances are that *even if the bear knows I am there*, I can move away from the bear without causing it to approach me. While moving away from a bear likely to have already detected me, I make plenty of noise, for instance singing out or breaking branches so that the bear can keep track of where I am, and thus avoid getting close by accident. Also, I don't want to run into another bear.
- I almost never worry about a bear following me with evil intent.
- Your best protection is to be in a group with at least 2 other people and preferably at least 4 other people, all within an arm's length of each other. If you are in a group of 5+ people, there is nearly 0 risk of being attacked. If you are in a group of just 3 people, the risk of attack is also very low if the bear has not been surprised at close range, and if you do not run in panic.
- If I encounter a bear that wants me to scram, for instance, a mother grizzly protecting small cubs, or any grizzly defending the carcass of a large animal (e.g., deer or moose), I do not immediately run away. Instead, I stand my ground while the bear is approaching me or violently threatening me. Not until the bear quits threatening and turns away from me, do I begin slowly retreating by walking sideways (so that I can glance at the ground to make sure I don't trip, then at the bear to see what it is doing, then back at the ground). If the bear lets me get at least 100 yards away without pursuing me, I might speed

up to a fast walk or jog, with little risk of the bear pursuing me. Was I to start running while within 50 yards of a bear, there is a chance it would chase me to exert dominance – much as a dog might chase a running person – in which case I might be bitten or swatted. Running almost never triggers a predatory attack, contrary to conventional wisdom.

- Bears rarely attack. Don't do anything to increase the probability. Don't provoke a peaceful bear or aggravate one that is merely nervous.
- When bears do attack, it is usually for one of four reasons: *1. Protection*, if the bear perceives you as a threat – e.g., a predator – to itself or its cubs (in the case of a mother bear). Although grizzly bears are notorious for protective attacks, black bears are not, unless you are with a dog that has been harassing the bear. *2. Defensive rivalry*: if the bear perceives you as a rival for its food, a mate, or another critical resource. Such attacks are made mainly by grizzly bears. *3. Offensive rivalry*: triggered if you are nearby guarding food or another attractant that the bear covets. Most rivalry attacks are by grizzly bears, e.g., if you are dressing out a moose or other game animal that you have just killed. *4. Predation*: if the bear perceives you as food. Grizzlies are about twice as likely as a black bear to treat you as prey. But this is not common with any kind of bear.
- I usually reduce the risk of attack by being prepared to use **bear-grade pepper spray** or a firearm. Furthermore, if a bear's aggression is: *1. Protective*: I try to set the bear at ease so that it trusts me. I try to appear harmless and submissive, for instance by moving away slowly, walking sideways, while not making eye contact except for momentary glances toward the bear, between glances at the ground to avoid tripping. But if the bear gets too aggressive, I will quit retreating and face it. If it calms down, I resume retreating. *2. Defensive rivalry*: If a bear is

guarding an animal carcass or other highly attractive food, I avoid showing interest in the food and retreat, walking sideways. Most of these attacks are also by grizzly bears, not black bears. *3. Offensive rivalry:* If I don't really want what the bear wants, I surrender it. Letting a bear bully me into surrendering food is not ideal, but I have done that to get to a safer position where I could retaliate, using bear-grade pepper spray if necessary. *4. Predatory:* If a bear persists in following me, perhaps circling me to get downwind, and keeps watching me, it might be either curious or predatory. If I then act aggressively and the bear backs off, acts defensive, or starts eating vegetation, chances are it is just curious. But if it seems unimpressed with my aggression, and keeps its eyes locked on me, I assume that this is one of the very rare bears that is predatory. So I become aggressive, approaching the bear, making loud abrupt harsh sounds (e.g., NO! GET OUT! LEAVE!), as I try to **get upwind** of the bear, prepared to blast it with bear-grade pepper spray or with a firearm.

Camping

- I surround my camp with an electric fence (6,000 – 10,000 volts) with intruder alarms.
- I avoid camping near a trail, feeding area, or other sites frequented by bears.
- I store all food and items that smell like food outside the tent in which I sleep. Bear-proof food containers are stored OUTSIDE my electric fence, on the downwind side, and attached to a bell so that if a bear tries to get my food, I am warned.

Warnings:

- A bear blasted with bear-strength pepper spray is very unlikely to retaliate. But a bear wounded with a bullet or arrow is as likely to retaliate as it is to flee.
- Grizzly bears are more vulnerable than black bears to pepper spray.
- I carry 2 cans of pepper spray so that if I have to use one, I still have a backup for protection until I can get to a bear-safe refuge.

Some of these precautions are now so widely known that you might think they are obvious to anyone with common sense. However, they were actually discovered slowly, over a period of centuries and decades. Despite not knowing most precautions during my youth, I camped in bear country with impunity for many years. So did Tim Treadwell from about June 1991 until his impunity ended in October 2003, which got him and Amie Huguenard killed.

You too can ignore most safety precautions most of the time, without being injured – much as you can safely drive without wearing a seatbelt for many years. But in the unlikely event of a car crash, a seatbelt can save you from injury or death. Likewise, in the event that you get near a bear, taking proper precautions can minimize the risk of being injured by the bear or of having to injure or kill the bear to protect yourself – a lesson that Treadwell learned too late.

Seeing is Believing

Two decades ago, when I first taught through the University of Alaska, one of the people who attended my class was a grey-bearded sport hunter named Warren. On the first day, he pulled me aside and announced that he probably knew more about bears than I did, but that he'd be polite and try not to steal my thunder.

Warren was like a lot of Alaskans. They bristle at anyone but a fellow hunter who even hints at knowing something about bears that they don't. For them, being *bear savvy* is a matter of pride, no matter how little first-hand experience they have. So I began each course by reminding attendees of an old saying: *"It isn't what you don't know that gets you into trouble; it's what you know that isn't so."* I admitted that this was something of which I reminded myself frequently in an effort to keep an open mind so that I didn't let ego blind me to learning from folks like Warren who might have seen something I haven't.

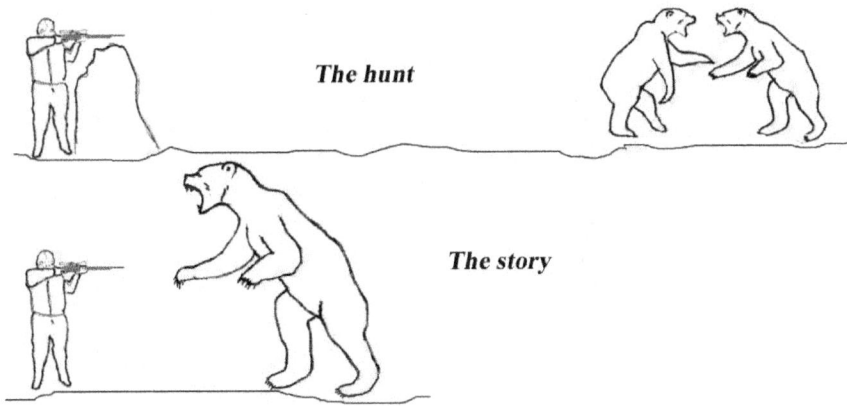

The hunt

The story

1.4: Embellishment is half the fun of telling hunting tales.

Long before I addressed the debate over whether fear of humans makes bears more likely or less likely to attack, or any other controversy about bear-human coexistence, I showed video footage of scores of bear-bear and bear-human interactions. The class watched selected interactions at normal speed, then in slow motion, identifying bear gestures, postures, facial expressions, vocalizations and other sounds. I compared among video clips where bears were violently protective of cubs and identified features in common with such events. I then compared those with clips of bears that were defending food, or that were merely frightened and warning or pleading with another bear or human to leave them alone.

Near the end of that course so long ago, Warren apologized for assuming that he was an expert on bear behavior. He admitted having learned far more than he thought possible from the many encounters documented in my video footage. His total prior experience amounted to a few brief encounters. Most of what he thought of as his own knowledge was second-hand or tenth-hand from reading or listening to people whose firsthand experience often extended little beyond hunting bears, and whose stories were garnished with misinterpretation, exaggeration, or fabrication.

1.5: Bear viewers on the eastern coast of Katmai National Park. This adult female grizzly is passing by just a few yards in front of them without obvious concern. This is typical at Katmai where unhunted bears have learned to trust people, and where there is an abundance of nutrient-rich wild foods such as salmon.

I wasn't sure what Warren actually retained from my class until a week or two after it ended. Around 4 am on a Sunday morning, my phone rang. It was Warren, announcing that the class had just saved his life and a friend's. They'd spent the pre-dawn hours in a tree-stand over bait, hoping that it would attract black bears so that each of them could kill one. Instead, their bait attracted three grizzlies, each of which looked almost tall enough to reach up and pull the men out of their tree – "or to knock it over," Warren chuckled.

Warren's friend was terrified and wanted to start shooting so that they could kill the bears before the bears could kill them – just as he'd read about someone doing in *Outdoor Life* or one of the more lurid "sportsman" magazines. However, there was little chance that the two men could kill or cripple all three bears before the bears could escape or attack. No one in his right mind wants to follow a wounded grizzly into a dense forest. And provoking an attack would almost certainly result in one or both men being injured or killed. At that point, the bears were still over fifty yards away. Were they not to discover that people were nearby before they got to the bait, about five yards from the men, the bears might react violently, perhaps attacking out of fear. To avoid that, Warren followed my advice, insisting that they immediately alert the grizzlies to their presence by talking softly. While the bears hung back, watching, both men quietly descended from the tree and walked away, with their bear-grade pepper spray ready for instant use. They escaped without harm to themselves or to the bears.

Because grizzly vs. black bears sometimes reacts differently during a close encounter, it's essential that you learn to distinguish them. Here are a few tips that will make it easier to tell them apart.

Grizzly/Brown Bears vs. Black Bears

When North America was first explored by Europeans, they encountered *Ursus americanus*, which were variously called baribels, black bears, or *blackies*, although some individuals were brown, tan, grey, or reddish (cinnamon). Explorers moving inland from the Caribbean or Pacific coasts also soon encountered grizzly bears. But explorers moving inland from the Atlantic did not encounter grizzlies until they crossed the Mississippi River. Few English-speaking people knew of grizzlies on this continent until they were reported by the Lewis & Clark expedition in 1804.

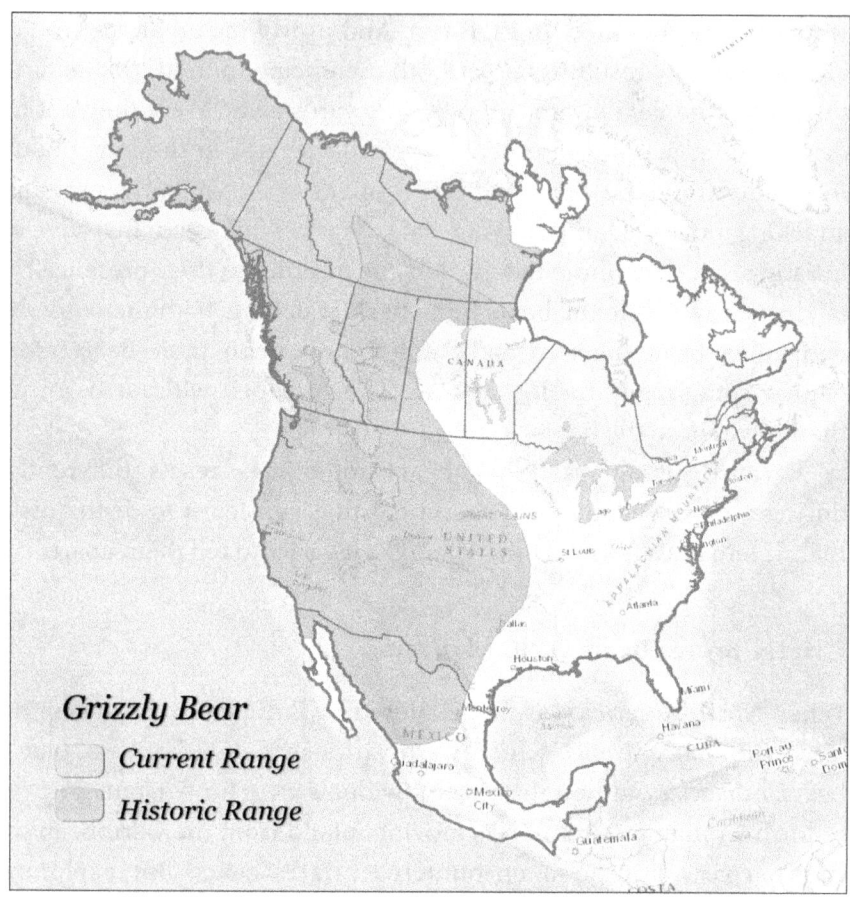

1.6: Current and historic distributions of *Ursus arctos* grizzly/brown bears in North America. usgs.gov/media/images/historical-and-current-grizzly-bear-range-north-america

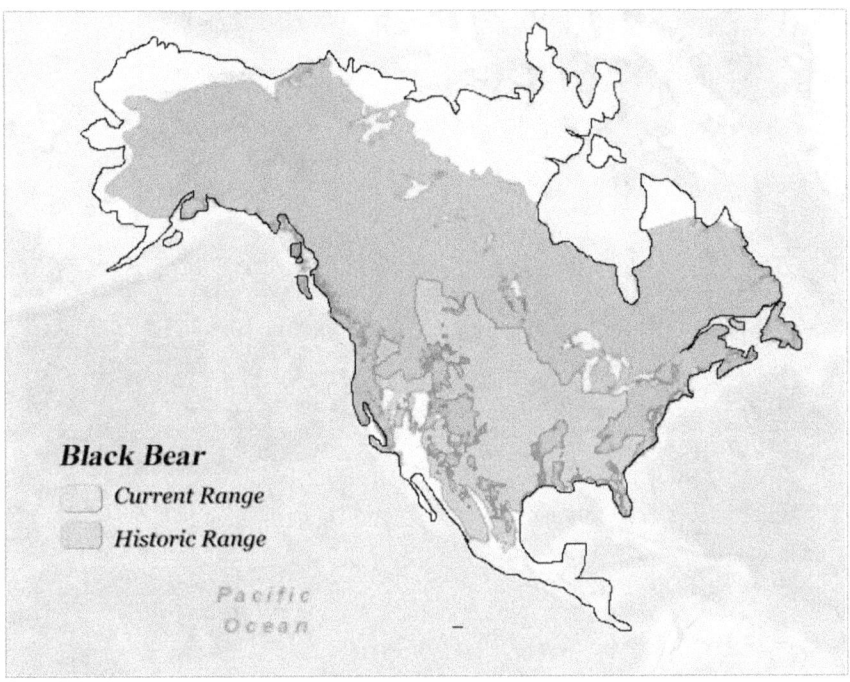

1.7: Current and historic distributions of *Ursus americanus* black/blackie bears in North America. Garshelis, D.L., Scheick, B.K., Doan-Crider, D.L., Beecham, J.J. & Obbard, M.E. 2016. *Ursus americanus. The IUCN Red List of Threatened Species* 2016: e.T41687A114251609. https://dx.doi.org/10.2305/IUCN.UK.2016-3. RLTS.T41687A45034604.en. Accessed on 03 February 2023.

Grizzlies tend to have more of a shoulder hump than blackies. Blackies tend to have more difference in coloration between the muzzle and the head. Where grizzlies and blackies share the same habitat, grizzlies tend to be at least half-again as large as blackies of the same age and sex. Polar bears have a medium size shoulder hump and are uniform white in color (range: snow white to cream or old ivory yellowish white).

1.8: Profiles of American bears. *Row 1*: Adult male black bear and a two-year old male. *Row 2:* Adult male brown bears (often darker than females and juveniles) *Row 3*: Mother brown bear followed by her 2-year-old cub. *Row 4:* Adult polar bears.

Unfortunately, naming each multi-colored species according to a single color has caused considerable confusion, especially in warmer more open habitats where both species could be brown or a lighter color. One the one hand, people have mistaken a light-colored black bear for a grizzly and panicked unnecessarily. One panicked woman tripped, fell and was permanently crippled! On the other hand, hunters have shot a grizzly bear thinking it was a light-colored black bear. To minimize such confusion, I usually refer to all North American *U. arctos* as "grizzlies." When it is necessary to distinguish salmon-fed *arctos* bears from those with little access to salmon, I refer to the former as "salmon-grizzlies" or as "brownies," by contrast to "salmon-scarce grizzlies" which include grizzlies in Alaska's interior and on the Arctic coast.

1.9: Juvenile grizzly bear and adult black bear of similar body size. Note the grizzly's much larger shoulder hump.

1.10: Grizzly bear (left) and black bear (right). Although the adult black bear was smaller, it was more aggressive and dominated the adolescent grizzly.

1.11: A so-called "glacier" or "blue" color phase of the black bear. This is a stuffed bear whose photo I inserted against a glacial background.

Grizzly or Brown Bear?

When explorers encountered *Ursus arctos* on the Pacific coast, at least the Russians would have recognized them as the same Eurasian species known as *brown bears* in English, *oso bruno* in Spanish, and *buryy medved* in Russian. But the North American variety differed in that the color of each hair was not uniform along the length of its shaft, as in much of Eurasia, but had a lighter-colored tip. Such hair tips have been labeled as "frosted," "brindled," "hoary," or "grizzled" in other mammals. Hence, the name *grizzled* or *grizzly* bear.

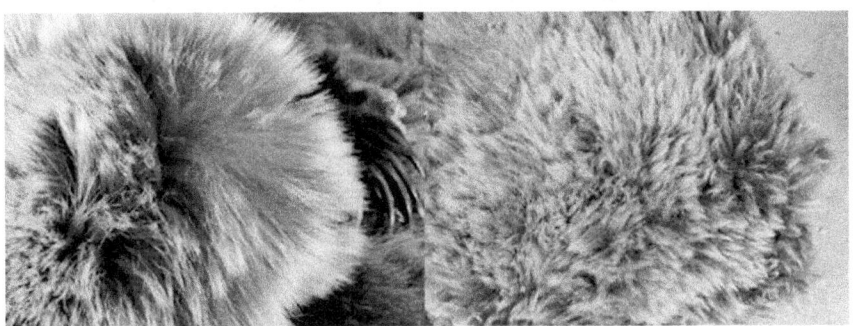

1.12: Grizzly pelts: "Grizzling" or lightening of hair tips is much more extreme and common for the interior bears (left) than for those on the coast (right), where they are often referred to as "brown bears."

As explorers moved from the Atlantic coast across the Mississippi River and ascended it to the Missouri River and beyond west into the Rocky Mountains, they encountered grizzlies and blackies of various colors. In relatively arid habitats, with few trees, where bears were often exposed to strong sunlight, light colors are advantageous to both bear species because they reflect away more heat. This was true all the way north to the Beaufort Sea of the Arctic Ocean, where summers are short but can be hot due to around-the-clock sunlight. Bears of both species can be white, tan, blond, reddish, chocolate, or blackish. Rare black bears with frosted hair are called glacier bears or blue bears.

Eventually, the term "grizzly" was applied to all North American *arctos* bears from coast to coast as Anglos annexed the center and western side of the continent, and English became the predominant language in both America and Canada. The term "brown bear" was retained only in Alaska where *arctos* bears with access to abundant salmon tend to have dark brown fur without distinctively light hair tips, although it's not uncommon to see fur with just slight lightening of the tips, perhaps due to sun bleaching.

Behavioral and anatomical differences between Alaska's salmon-grizzlies vs. salmon-scarce grizzlies seem to be due less to genetic differences than to cultural and dietary differences. Salmon-grizzlies consume much more protein and lipid, usually in the form of salmon, resulting in larger bodies and higher reproductive rates, as well as greater tolerance for proximity with fellow bears. Greater tolerance minimizes social strife while foraging near one another at prime fishing sites on salmon streams or on marine mammal carcasses. Although salmon-scarce grizzly bears (like black bears and polar bears) also aggregate to feed on highly concentrated food sources, such as a whale carcass that has washed up on shore, or at a garbage dump, it's not clear that salmon-scarce grizzlies do this as readily or as tolerantly as salmon-grizzlies. All records which I've found on California grizzlies suggest that they were as social as Alaska's salmon-grizzlies, in keeping with the (historic) abundance of salmon in some California watersheds up until the mid-1800s. The last California grizzly was killed in 1926.

This "grizzly" vs. "brown bear" distinction is less about ecology and behavior toward humans than it is about the bragging rights of hunters. Someone who kills a large interior-grizzly doesn't want the achievement disrespected just because even a large salmon-scarce-grizzly is commonly smaller than a medium-size salmon-grizzly or a large black bear in California or Pennsylvania.

* * *

Once you know how to distinguish between salmon-scarce grizzly bears vs. salmon-grizzly/brown bears, as well as between them an black bears, you can better understand differences in how you can best behave during a close encounter. Some of the safety tips I've listed above might now seem obvious because those ones have been wildly publicized since the early or mid-1980s. However, that knowledge did not appear by magic or divine inspiration. It was discovered step-by-step over many decades. This memoir recalls some of my own discoveries, especially discoveries about living in harmony with bears that ran counter to conventional wisdom during the 1970s. Unfortunately, conventions persist long after they become obsolete. Hence, some of the ideas presented here remain controversial, although their validity has been proven time and time again, beginning in the late 1800s and early 1900s, as described by Enos Mills in his book *The Grizzly* (1919). Mills was an expert naturalist and wildlife viewing guide who spent countless hours watching grizzlies in Colorado's Rocky Mountains. He was also a prime figure in the creation of Rocky Mountains National Park. Not only was his book my first "bible" about bear behavior, but I got my own start in life and as a bear watcher just south of that Park, right after WWII, as recalled in Chapter 2.

Multimedia for Chapter 1.

2

BEAR VALLEY

2.1: One of the cabins in which I lived as a youth.

Was I Nearly "Baby Food" for a Bear?

S ome bears might be maneaters. Fortunately, I wasn't yet a man the first time I encountered a bruin. I was still a toddler, playing safely behind the railings of our cabin porch, 8,000 feet high in the Rocky Mountains. My father was mining gold less than a hundred yards away. When he returned home that afternoon for a cup of coffee, tracks on the sandy ground revealed that our garbage pit had attracted a bear, which passed within a few feet of the porch where I was crawling around or riding a rocking-horse.

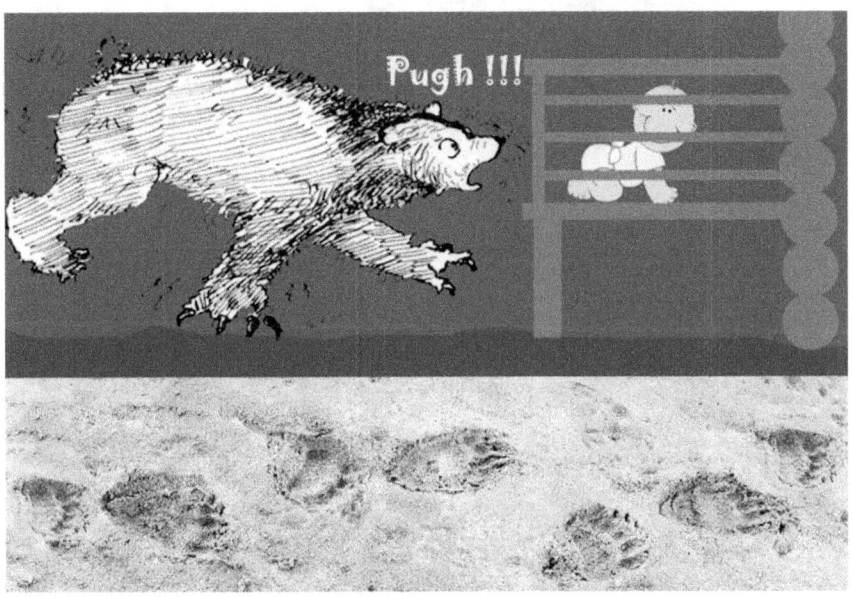

2.2: My first bear encounter occurred during infancy when a bear investigated me as I was playing on our cabin porch. Although my folks never saw the bear, they saw its tracks.

I don't know what the bear's intent was, but even if it was one of those very rare predatory bruins, one sniff of my diapers might have ruined its appetite for "baby food." It wandered off without bothering me in the least. Nevertheless, fearing that the bear might return in a less benign mood, my folks became even more careful about not letting me outdoors alone.

By the time I was a year old, I'd spend hours at a time rocking, sometimes falling asleep on my wooden steed. By age three, I'd worn out my first rocking horse and graduated to a larger one.

2.3: Age 3, still rocking away (photo by Joyce Stringham).

2.4: Age 4, with my first sister, Christine, age 2, and our
dog Chip (photo by Joyce Stringham).

2.5: By that time, grizzlies were rare in Colorado, but blackies were and are still abundant.

Given my passion for "horses" and my love of dressing up like a cowboy, my parents might have predicted that I'd aim for a career as a rodeo bronc buster. But they would never have guessed that over the decades which followed, I'd devote my life to researching and conserving bears.

Chronology

Given that my memoir is organized by topic, it jumps around in time. To avoid confusion about the sequence of events, here is a timeline:

- 1947: My father returned from WWII and we moved onto a gold claim in the Rocky Mts. My first bear encounter.
- 1962: Encounters in Bear Valley, California Sierra Mts.
- 1963: Encountered a black bear and a raccoon near Knights Ferry in California.

- 1966: Encountered black bears and a grizzly in Montana's Rocky Mts. Saw people feeding LSD-laced sugar cubes to bears.
- 1969: Awarded BSc degree in Biological Oceanography/Marine Ecology. Assisted with a black bear study on the California coast.
- 1970: Observed grizzly and black bears on Alaska's Kenai Peninsula, between bouts of research on moose.
- 1972: Studied brown/grizzly bears at Brooks River, Katmai National Park. Book *Nearly Breakfast for a Grizzly Bear.*
- 1973: I mentored three orphaned bear cubs until they could fend for themselves in the Alaska wilderness (June-Aug). Book *Beauty Within the Beast.*
- 1973-1975: Researched wildlife in the Tirolean Alps of Austria
- 1974: Awarded MSc degree in Wildlife Management.
- 1976: Research on grizzly bear behavioral and population ecology. I collaborated with the Craighead team which worked in Yellowstone National Park and with the Jonkel team which worked at the Montana-Canada border. I assisted Chuck Jonkel in his Border Grizzly research, trapping black and grizzly bears to mark and measure them, before releasing them again.
- 1978-83: I also assisted fellow grad students who were studying black bears in the Great Smoky Mountains National Park. I once came eyeball to eyeball with a bear in its den (as told in this book.)
- 1984: Awarded Ph.D. in Behavioral & Population Ecology
- 1985-1986: Post-doctoral research on black bears in New York's Adirondack Park
- 1987-1989: Assessed impacts on Vermont black bears by the ski industry.
- 1989-1990: Assessed potential impacts on Vermont black bears by a proposed natural gas pipeline.

- 1990-1991: Taught at Salish-Kootenai College on the Flathead Indian Reservation, Montana. Observed grizzly and black bears in the Mission Mts.
- 1991-1992: Taught at Blackfeet Community College, Blackfeet Indian Reservation, Montana.
- 1992-1993: Directed the Environmental Office of the Blackfeet Indian Nation. Observed grizzly and black bears in Glacier National Park.
- 1994: Returned home to Alaska and worked on the polar bear management team of the US Fish & Wildlife Service.
- 1994-1996: Black bear research in Southeast Alaska.
- 1997: Grizzly research at Ivanoff Bay on the Alaska Peninsula.
- 1998-2019: Grizzly research at Katmai National Park.
- 2000-2002: Taught course *Bears & Bear Safety* and *Alaska Mammals*, U of Alaska.
- 2004, 2013-2022: Grizzly and black bear research, interspersed with guiding viewers at Alaska's Diving Bear Cove, west of Cook Inlet.
- 2021-2025: Research on grizzlies at Chinitna Bay.

Many years passed before my second bear encounter. In the meantime, my folks sold the gold mine and my father returned to college where he earned his Master's degree in organic chemistry – the field in which he worked for the rest of his professional life. Along the way, my parents birthed four daughters, ranging from two to ten years younger than myself. After several more years living in Colorado, we moved to the town of Modesto in California's Central Valley where summertime temperatures sometimes reached 120 degrees. It was like moving from the outskirts of Heaven to the outskirts of Hell. In place of lofty mountains, we were stuck in the flatlands, surrounded by endless fields of wine grapes and other crops. Not ideal surroundings for a young man craving adventure.

During the hottest months each year, my family spent most of our free time in the irrigation canals that crisscrossed the agricultural community. We swam, dove, tanned until we were dark brown, and raised hell. Finally, in August of each year, we escaped from the oppressive heat of those agricultural lands for a cooler week of camping on the Pacific Coast or in the Sierra mountains.

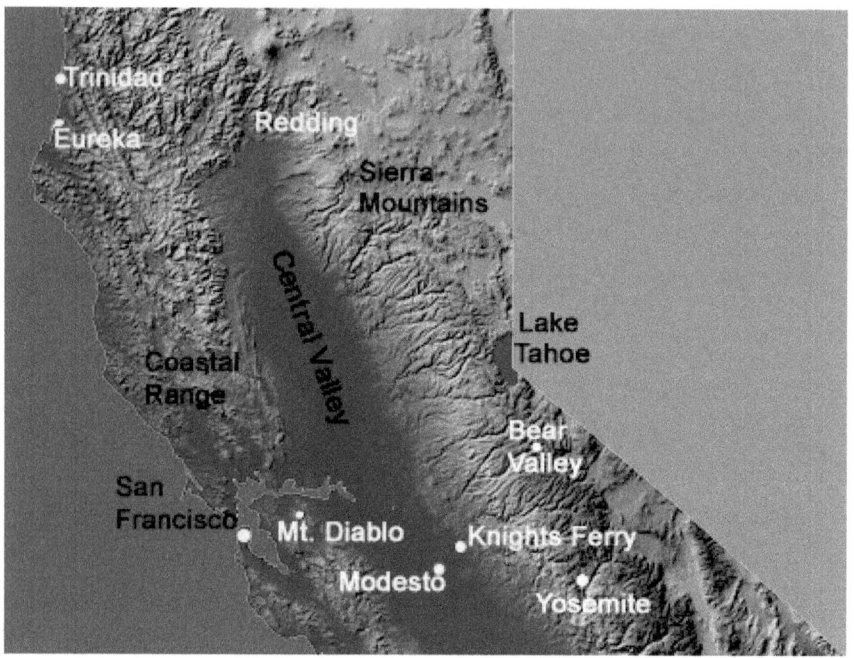

2.6: Map of California's Central Valley and surrounding mountains. I first got to know bears on the western slope of the Sierra Range between Lake Tahoe and Yosemite (Getty image).

In 1962, when I was 16, Dad and Mom chose the Mokelumne Wilderness, north of Yosemite National Park, about two-thirds of the way to Lake Tahoe. At the trailhead, our whole family donned backpacks. We climbed over a high ridge and down into Bear Valley, which emptied into the Mokelumne River Gorge. It was easy terrain with a good trail. But it was quite a chore to haul enough food and gear for two parents and five kids. Most of my siblings were too young to carry more than their own clothes. My father and I were the family mules, each hefting at least 60 pounds.

2.7: Dad fly fishing for trout.

Within a few hours, we had reached a fine camping spot. It was in a dry dusty meadow, covered with sparse ankle-high grass. A cobalt lake shimmered nearby, mirroring mountain slopes and puffy cumulus clouds scattered across a pale blue sky.

Our tents were quickly set up. Sleeping bags were rolled out and air mattresses were inflated. Armloads of branches were gathered for the evening fire when Mom would cook supper and Dad would tell ghost stories – ghosts of the mountain men and of the Indians who had once roamed the high Sierras; ghosts of men who had sought golden riches but found granite graves

First, though, Dad took his fly rod and went to try the stream whose clear gurgling waters whet our appetites for crisply-fried trout. Mom headed toward the lake, her arm curled around her easel and a box of watercolor pigments. Her paintings would preserve images of the day long after our memories had faded.

Meanwhile, I took off hiking and was soon following a game trail that paralleled a creek flowing downhill toward Mokelumne River Gorge. Although California and many other states have numerous geographic features referring to bears, such as Bear Valley in this case, few of those features are still frequented by bears. Had Dad known that this area was an exception, he would never have allowed me to wander off on my own. But ignorant folk frolic where their wiser brethren fear to tread.

Blithely unaware that I was minutes away from my next close encounter, I interrupted my hike to watch a foot-long rainbow trout feeding in an eddy of the creek. The flecks of red and peach on its flanks were invisible. Only its brown back was exposed. Except for the slight movement of its fins and gills, the fish looked like just another sunken stone.

That triggered my own eagerness to catch trout. I'd neglected to bring my fishing pole. So I rigged one from a pine branch, using yards of the monofilament line and a hook that I carried for emergencies.

I dug up a worm and was about to impale it on my hook when my eye was caught by movement in the brush fifty yards downstream. A black bear burst out of the willows and charged into the clear, cold creek. Chasing fish, it splashed through the belly deep stream. Gleaming rooster-tails of water shot high on each side of its back. Sun-pierced droplets of agua split the light prismatically into a multitude of colors. Each droplet was a miniature star turned red or violet, blue or green as though dopplered by the speed of its flight away from or toward me.

"Yes!" I screamed ecstatically but silently. "Yes!" I was thrilled. Then, terrified. I was in the bear's path! It could run right over me!

Petrified, I couldn't move – which was supposedly the right response. Flight could be seen. If a bear didn't discover me until it was a few yards away, its shock and fear might trigger an attack. When it comes to self-defense, the "Law of the wild" prevails – not "Shoot first and ask questions later" – but claw and bite first. Or so I had been informed by a magazine story about bears, based less on knowledge than on myth. (Since there were no books on bear safety back in the 1960s, few people had any clue about how to behave to avoid trouble – except to immediately kill the animal. Better safe than sorry.)

2.8: Splash as the bear struck out, trying to catch a fish.

The bear's charge stopped five yards away. I was downwind, hidden in the shade of a ponderosa pine, screened by its huge roots and by shrubs, frozen with a combination of fear and excitement. How long until the bear found me? How long until an eddy of swirling air wafted my scent to the huge carnivore?

Hardly able to breathe, much less to move, I shivered. Not from a chill. Temperatures soared toward the nineties even in the shade. The bear cruised the pool. Its head submerged looking for fish. It raced futilely after prey. Finally, it got lucky. One of the fleeing trout sought to escape across an inch-deep riffle. Scraping bottom, nearly stranding, the fish trashed furiously. Just as the trout reached slightly deeper water and surged ahead, the bear took two lightening bounds and pinned the trout with its hand-like forepaw, crushing the fish against gravel. Powerful ursine jaws lifted the struggling rainbow skywards. Blood streamed crimson down the trout's mangled body, then over the bear's black lips, dripping into the creek as the bear lumbered ashore.

Dropped onto the dusty forest duff, with its scattering of rusty pine needles, the fish flopped weakly toward the creek until pinned again by five sharp claws. The trout's head disappeared with an audible crunch into the ursine maw. A taste of dust and fish and blood drifted downwind to my tongue.

The bear glanced from side to side. Another bite and its surroundings were again surveyed. The bear's head stopped moving. Its body tensed. Its nose lifted. Its mouth opened and closed slowly, tongue flicking in and out several times, catching airborne odors in saliva, and pulling them back into the vomeronasal chemosensory organ in the roof of its mouth, trying to detect any lurking enemy.

2.9: Capturing a trout, the bear walked ashore to devour it.

Had it finally detected me? Had I more than just seconds to live? Racked by fear, the grumbling of my bowels reverberated like thunder. Storm waves of blood beat against my ear drums.

I feared that the bear could hear those sounds too. Yet it never looked in my direction. Its attention was focused downstream. Was an enemy approaching?

Minutes passed. The night-dark animal relaxed. Its head shook, and then its body, a mighty thrashing from nose to tail. Water from its fur sprayed in every direction. Stray droplets sprinkled me.

The bear's head dipped a final time, then rose. The trout's tail hung between the bruin's ebony lips, then slipped out of sight down its throat.

Gently as smoke, the hairy angler was gone too.

My shivers magnified into shudders. They racked me from chest to ankles. Earlier surges of adrenaline may have exhausted my blood sugar. I felt lucky not to have been mauled. I wanted to whoop for joy, feeling lucky to have survived, sure the bear would have attacked if it had detected me. Although we had lived in bear country during my infancy, we'd long since moved to areas without bears, so the subject of bear safety had never arisen in family discussions. At that time, my perception of bears was entirely colored by lurid magazine stories.

Body gradually returning to normal, I emerged cautiously from my hiding place between tree roots and trunk. Stepping out onto the sunny trail, the sudden heat made me shiver again, just for a second. Cramped muscles compelled a mighty stretch.

God, but it was good to be alive! Laughter bubbled through me. I could hardly wait to get back to camp and report my adventure.

Fate, however, had other plans. I had company again. A few hundred yards down the trail toward the Gorge was a much larger bear. No wonder the first one had disappeared!

I quickly surveyed my options. Soon it would reach this spot on the trail. Its nose, far superior to that of a bloodhound, couldn't miss my odor. If the bear followed my spoor, could I escape? Where could I take refuge?

Running back up the trail toward camp would be foolish. Camp was two miles away uphill. I'd be seen and could be chased down within a hundred yards – if the bear was so-inclined. I had to try sneaking away, even if that just delayed the inevitable. I was down-wind of the bear, so it might not smell me until it got closer to this spot. When that happened, it could quickly track me down and attack, unless I was out of reach. How? Climb a tree? I was surrounded by forest. But most of the trees were Ponderosa pine, with few reachable branches. Anyway, the bear was a better climber. Of trees. But what about sheer rock walls? Could it climb them? Could I? I had no skills as a rock climber but had good upper body strength from years of competitive swimming and gymnastics.

2.10: As a gymnast, my specialty was trampoline. Here I was landing a double-front flip (photo by Jeanette Stringham).

Nearby a pale grey granite cliff rose several hundred feet above the trail. Ducking low among shoulder-high brush to remain hidden, I hurried away and began climbing. Bounding like a deer, I dodged among rocks and leaped deadfall, fueled with the energies of youth and fear. But energy, like youth, wanes quickly. Far short of the cliff, the thrust of my legs faded. They turned rubbery. My pace slowed to a stumble. I staggered, then collapsed in the shade of another large ponderosa. My breath came in great shuddering gasps. My right side ached like I'd been mule-kicked. Using the tree for support and cover, I peered around its trunk toward the trail. The bear was now less than a hundred yards from the spot where I'd left the trail. Discovery could be only minutes away.

Still gasping for air, I ducked low again amid the shrubs and stumbled up the slope. It had steepened to forty degrees. Legs pumping weakly, I was hauled toward the cliff by my arms, pulling on shrubs and tree branches.

2.11: Shortly after the first black bear left, a larger one appeared.

Finally, I was near the cliff's base. Fifty feet above me was a shelf that looked wide enough to walk along. So far, so good.

The bear still seemed unaware of me. It advanced slowly up the trail, feeding leisurely on berries. It grasped a berry-laden branch in one forepaw, held the branch crossways to its mouth, just behind the canines, then yanked its head sideways, pulling off berries and leaves together. This happened several times before the bruin switched to plucking berries off individually with its prehensile lips.

I reached the ledge. Roughly two feet wide, it crossed the cliff face for a few hundred yards before reaching a grassy slope. An ideal escape route. Moving forward, I accidentally knocked a stone off the ledge. It fell, and knocked off more stones, creating a tiny landslide that startled the bear. It looked up toward me. Standing erect like a person, its ears were forward, arms hanging loosely. Its head turned to the side, back up the trail. Several times, its jaw sank a few inches, then closed. Its tongue flicked in and out several times, as though licking its nostrils to wet them so that they could pick up scent more readily, or perhaps licking scent off its nose so it could taste the odors too. The bruin dropped to the ground and faced up the trail toward where I had crossed, huffing nervously.

Although it might now have my scent, I hoped it wouldn't follow me. Yet, no sooner had that thought crossed my mind then the bear burst into a gallop. With each rocking-horse bound, shoulders rising high then sinking as the hindquarters rose then fell, it leaped ten to fifteen feet per stride – up the trail. Away from me!

Where there were two bears, there'd be more. No wonder they called this Bear Valley. To avoid any more encounters on my way to the Mokelumne Gorge, I had to stay off the valley floor trails. I'd best travel along the top of the ridge above the cliff. To get there, I could follow this ledge as far as possible. Once on the grassy slope, I could climb to the top of the ridge and follow that. The ledge was like having a paved highway leading just where I wanted to go.

Well, the best-laid plans .... After ascending the steeply sloping ledge a couple of hundred feet, I was within fifty yards of the grass. The ledge turned a corner, then stopped. A gap of about five feet separated me from where the ledge continued a body length below. One body length out of the fifty separating me from the ground.

Sure that I could make the jump safely, I quickly did so. Cocky, proud for having overcome my fear, I continued ahead certain that I could handle anything I encountered. Well, not quite anything. Rounding the next corner, I faced another gap, this one more than twenty feet across. Not even a mountain goat could jump it.

I retreated to the smaller gap and gauged my chances of returning across it. The only way to make it back would be to run, leap and catch the ledge under my arms, then muscle myself up. Had there been no cliff below me, I'd have tried it. But with more than a hundred feet of freefall, any slip would be fatal.

"When in doubt, sit down and think it out," as the saying goes. Good advice. I couldn't go forward or back. I probably couldn't descend the cliff face. Going down a cliff, it's hard to find secure toe holds and to chart your route from one set of hand and toe holds to the next. Going up offered much better visibility. The sloping rock wall rose only another sixty feet. It would be easy to ascend, and I was able to plot a return route if I needed to retreat to the ledge.

Above that wall was a talus slope a hundred feet high whose top leveled out onto the grassy ridge I'd been trying to reach. Taking that route would be risky. I thought about just sitting on the ledge and waiting for rescue. But days could pass before anyone found me. Meanwhile, my family would be terrified. I couldn't wait. The sky was darkening and a few drops of rain had already spattered me. If a full-blown rainstorm hit, I'd be soaked and chilled. Even if hypothermia didn't kill me, I could get careless and roll off the ledge. This escape route would have to do.

Ascending the wall was as easy as climbing a ladder, and took just a couple of minutes. Looking down, I was half-shocked to see that the bear had returned. It was standing bipedally on the ledge below me, looking up. Was it just curious? Could it be predatory? Bearanoid thoughts shot through my mind. Was it going to climb up after me, knock me off the cliff, then climb to the base of the cliff and lunch on my carcass?

No sooner did the bear's eyes meet mine, then it began rhythmically huffing, snapping its jaws, and moaning. Not recognizing that as a sign of anxiety, I misinterpreted it as a threat comparable to the way dogs bark and snap their teeth. I was relieved when the bear turned away and walked back along the ledge, leaving me alone. I hung there on the cliff for several minutes, waiting to see what the bear would do. Then I resumed climbing, sure that it was my only option for survival, and daring not still be on the cliff face when the rain began.

So far, ascending over solid rock had been easy because its surface had been scoured clean by wind and rain. But the higher I climbed, and the shallower the slope of the bedrock, the more sand had accumulated. Those grains could act like tiny ball bearings, destroying my grip on the rock face and launching me into space.

To cross that area, I had to hold on with one hand, while I swept the rock surface clean with the other hand. I continued climbing this way up another thirty feet before I reached a section of cliff that sloped gently enough to retain a covering of talus – slabs and chunks of rock broken off the cliff by ice wedging. During autumn, rain water seeped into cracks. When that water froze, it expanded so powerfully that it split off layers of rock and splintered them into pieces called talus, ranging in size from pebbles to boulders. This slope was covered with them more than a foot deep, providing no grip for a climber. Anything I grabbed would just pull free and slide off the cliff, possibly taking me with it.

Rain drops were still infrequent, but between them and sweat, my clothes were damp. The wind was picking up and I was tiring. Once again, it was time to do or die. I had to either find a way through the talus slope or fall hundreds of feet to become food for worms and bears.

It dawned on me then that the talus was lying on bedrock, just as the sand had been lower down. Digging into the talus with one hand, while gripping bed rock with the other, I dug through a foot of talus, sweeping it off the cliff face and out into space.

At first, I tried digging holes down to the rock where I could place my hands and feet. But the loose dirt and gravel kept sliding into each hole as fast as I dug it out. My only option was to leave the talus debris in place and burrow down through it with one hand. Once I found something solid, I could hold on, then extend the other arm and burrow with it.

I rarely had a grip for more than one hand and arm at a time. Talus slid into my hand-dug holes so quickly that I could seldom find solid footing for my toes. So it was hold on with my right arm, dig with the left, pull myself upwards with my left arm, then hold there while digging with my right arm. And so on for the next hour or so. Ascending the slope was almost like doing one-armed pullups – although fortunately not against my full body weight. I'd gotten to the point where I *could* do one-armed pullups on the still rings in gymnastics. So I had little trouble with this method of ascent. The biggest challenge was to keep cool and focused. Only eagles could afford to slip here.

Suddenly it was over. I reached a narrow cleft in the cliff where there was no talus, just clean bedrock. Placing my feet against one side of the cleft and my back against the other, I quickly ascended the final fifty feet to the crest of the cliff, where the forest began. Gripping the roots of a small ponderosa, I pulled myself onto the grass and lay there panting.

Minutes passed before I realized that I was not alone. A bear materialized out of the nearby forest. It looked like the one which had followed me onto the cliff. Same body color with a similar blaze of white fur on its chest. It was standing just yards away. I was still lying in the grass, one cheek against the ground. I didn't dare move. I didn't even dare stare at the bear. As I shut my eyes to mere slits and watched the bear, my muscles began shivering. The bear nosed my body, then my face. When its nose touched mine ever so gently, it tickled. A sneeze exploded from my face.

2.12: The bear came back again.

The black bear whirled around and away, bursting into a gallop as it wove between trees. Earlier, the first bear had disappeared like wind-puffed smoke. This one disappeared like a tornado-blown leaf.

Stunned, I lay there, still gasping for breath. For more than two hours I had been stuck on the cliff face, knowing that any wrong move would be fatal. Next, I'd been terrified while being sniffed by a bear. Yet all of a sudden, it seemed like just a lark, as though the danger had been imaginary. Intellectually, I believed the danger had been all too real. Yet once I was again on safe ground, and the bear had fled, I could hardly take the danger seriously. Suddenly, I was laughing, violently, explosively, almost giddy with relief.

That was my first time being touched by a bear. Its only ferocity had been in my imagination. This experience contradicted all the stories I'd read or heard about bears hunting humans or attacking at the slightest excuse. It was my first hint of how willing most bears are to live and let live with humans.After my climbing ordeal and bearanoia, I was hot and soaked with sweat. My mouth was sticky with dried saliva and I was desperate for water. As soon as I found another creek free of bears, I stripped off and jumped in. As I recall, the rock there was sandstone. It was riddled with potholes, some just a foot or so across, others bigger than a bathtub. The water was clear and cool. Better yet, it had an exquisite, slightly sweet flavor, better than any other water or soda pop I'd ever tasted. I sank under water and carefully sucked it in through lips and skin.

Fishing Frolic

My next bear encounter occurred a year later, in 1963, on another weekend when the thermometer strained past 100°. We declared that it was too hot for our normal Saturday yard work. Piling into the family station wagon, we drove from Modesto toward the Sierra foothills where it would be marginally cooler. The vehicle was an oven, made bearable only by the breeze flowing in through the windows. Sweat dripping down our faces dried to a salt crust on our skin.

Our destination was a park near the historic town of Knight's Ferry, complete with an old grist mill and the longest covered wooden-bridge west of the Mississippi River.

Years before, someone had climbed one of the large oaks that arched over the stream and hung a thick rope with a horizontal stick tied at the bottom. A person could stand on the stick while swinging out over the stream, before dropping off into the water, trying to make a splash big enough to soak everyone on shore. Dad and I, however, sometimes used the swing more like a trapeze, turning flips after letting go.

We also threw double flips off a nearby cliff towering about forty feet above the river. Dad's favorite dive was the swan, with his back beautifully arched until just before he entered the water. Years later, when I coached diving for Texas A&M University, I was sad to see the loss of such aesthetic dives. Modern competition requires a knife-straight body that makes a minimum splash while slicing down into the water.

2.13: Salmon which a bear had caught and brought ashore, then left while it chased another fish.

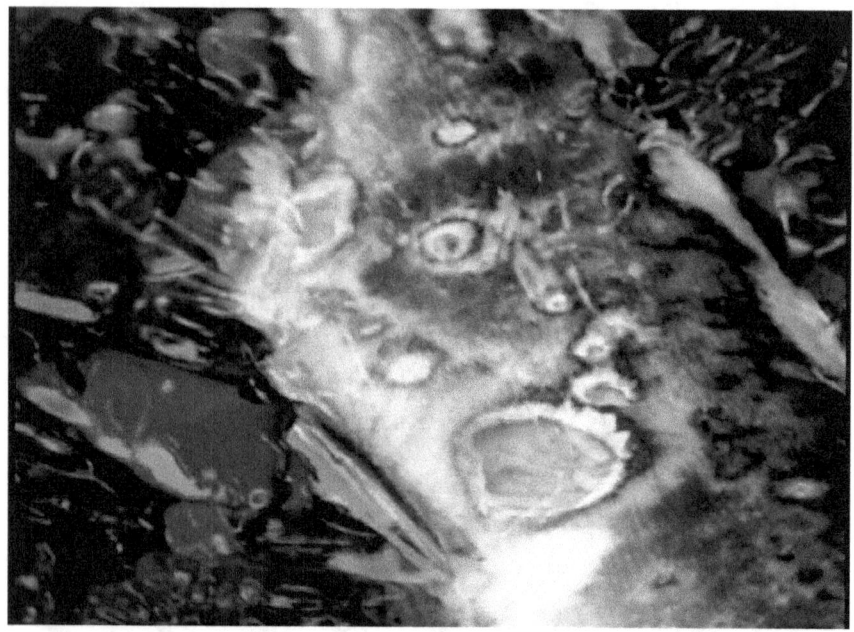

2.14: Salmon with ulcers on its flank from injuries while swimming upstream from the sea, or from fighting other males.

2.15: Blackie carrying a salmon ashore for lunch.

After lunch and a nap, we were ready to dive in again. But something stopped us abruptly. In the stream were the largest fish any of us had ever seen, each almost a yard long, and covered with pink patches which looked like ulcers. My father identified them as king salmon whose skin had been damaged against rocks while they swam more than a hundred miles upstream from the ocean to mate. With all the sores on their bodies, we thought they were too diseased to eat. The girls chased them around briefly, trying to catch them by hand until my father called a halt and told the girls to leave the fish alone so that they could finish spawning before they died.

2.16: Blackie resting beside creek amid salmon scraps.

Although my sisters desisted, a black bear did not. While my family splashed around near where we'd parked, I swam upstream, following a small school of salmon several hundred yards around a bed in the river. I was surprised to see a black bear on the stream-bank, miles from the nearest forest where black bears usually foraged. It had presumably followed the river downstream while hunting salmon.

After my previous summer's encounters in Bear Valley, I felt little fear of this bear and was content to watch as it plunged into the water, and bounded toward the salmon. Healthy fish could have easily escaped the bear, but these moribund ones could not. Within seconds, she had one in her jaws. Apparently, she didn't like an audience while she dined. Before starting to feed, she turned her back on me, as though afraid I'd demand a share of her prize.

By the time this bear caught another salmon, she was less concerned by my proximity than by the hot sun beating down on her black fur. Rather than leave the cool water, she found a shady spot, then lay down, mostly covered by water as she ate, again facing away from me. Over a period of about half an hour, this 200-pound carnivore consumed most of two fish, which together probably weighed nearly a tenth of her body weight. Finally satiated, she became playful, holding the remains of one fish in her jaws, violently shaking her head from side to side, before releasing the fish carcass so that it flew several yards off to one side. Then she leaped after it, like a dog playing with a chew toy, grabbed it again, and flung it once more. Now and then, she also used her forepaws to grasp what was left of a fish and throw it several yards.

Not until she waddled off into the brush did I swim back downstream and rejoin my family to share the news, and join in their fun.

Ransacking Raccoon

That night provided a different sort of wildlife encounter. I was suddenly awakened by something tugging my hair. Turning, I expected to see one of my sisters. No one was there. "Maybe it was my imagination," I thought. Yet soon my hair was pulled again, painfully.

Instantly my hand snapped back ... and hit a furry body. Whirling around, I saw a packrat tightrope running along the guyline that held my tent to a tree.

Why had it been pulling my hair? As I lay down again to sleep, I reached back to reposition my rolled-up jeans which I used for a pillow. My hand touched the leather belt; it felt strangely rough. Examining the leather with a flashlight, I saw where the rat had gnawed the belt almost in half. Why? Was it after salt left by my sweat? If so, the rat might come back again and again all night. To avoid that, I got up and dug salt out of the food box, then sprinkled it on the picnic table.

An hour or so later, we were awakened by a clang. Looking around, we saw nothing. I told Dad it was probably the packrat, returning for salt. We tried to go back to sleep, but soon the clangs resumed.

This time Dad got out of his sleeping bag and looked around camp. Moonlight revealed nothing. Yet when his flashlight illuminated the shrubs surrounding camp, he saw shining eyes much bigger than a rat's. At first, we thought it was a bear cub, presumably accompanied by its mother. Once it moved more into the light, however, we saw that it was a raccoon.

Now we understood. We'd picked a gallon of blackberries that afternoon. Mom had baked cobbler in the cast iron dutch oven. We'd eaten only half of it, saving the rest for breakfast. That remained in the dutch oven on the picnic table.

Dad switched off the flashlight and cautioned us to be silent. After about five minutes, the coon was back atop the table. It was no more than twenty pounds – too small and weak to lift the dutch oven lid by its handle. The coon instead grasped the lid by one edge and lifted that, tilting the lid nearly upright. As soon as it saw the cobbler, it let go of the lid and reached for the goodies – whereupon the lid slammed down on its hand. I winced just imagining the pain. This went on again and again, each time with the lid falling back into position with its handle upright. Finally, the coon lifted the lid so high that it flipped over upside down, again covering the pot, but with the handle inside. Now that the lid's handle was out of reach, the coon could no longer budge the lid. It churred loudly in frustration.

Sympathetic with the raccoon, Dad got up and scooped out a small cup of cobbler, sprinkling it with sugar for our furry guest. As we all lay in the tent watching, the raccoon returned and found his goodies. He became talkative, purring as though totally delighted at our offering. The purr of this raccoon was almost identical to that of a bear cub – testimony to the close genetic relationship between raccoons and bears.

Multimedia for Chapter 2.

3

PHANTOM GRIZZLY

3.1: Historic etching of "Grizzly" Adams, with his grizzly bear, Benjamin Franklin, from the 1860 *Hutchings' Illustrated California Magazine*

Nowadays, anyone even moderately versed in wildlife safety knows better than to leave food out on a picnic table or in a cooler where a bear or raccoon can help itself. But back in the 1960s, most folks were pretty clueless. At first, we were no exception. But we were beginning to learn, in large part due to the publication of insights by a handful of people who had been interacting with California bears dating since the mid-1800s – people whom I sought to emulate.

Several times during my teens, I hiked through the high Sierras, striding across meadows, then struggling up steep granite slopes. Once reaching the apex of some tall peak, I loved luxuriating as an alpine glow graced the wild landscape around me. I recall wondering what feet had trod these same trails before me

– black bears, grizzly bears, Indians, explorers, miners, or wannabes like me? I read numerous books about early Euro-American explorers such as James Fremont, as well as about prospectors and hunters. I was particularly fascinated by the stories of James Capen Adams, otherwise known as Grizzly Adams. As a teenager, steeped in bearanoia, I marveled at tales of his hunting prowess and courage against predators of such legendary ferocity and stamina, that couldn't be killed until riddled with bullets.

I also marveled at his success in capturing live grizzlies for zoos; for touring with one or more of them on display; and especially for taming two grizzlies – Lady Washington and Ben Franklin – which accompanied him as pack animals carrying his gear and supplies. Ben even protected Adams from another grizzly.

Back in the 1960s, I saw this as evidence of Adams' ability to dominate even such incredibly fierce animals. True, the California black bears which I'd encountered in 1962 and 1963 weren't the ravening demons portrayed by lurid magazine stories. However, I suspected that those black bears would have been more aggressive under other circumstances. Furthermore, I knew from the 1955 book *California Grizzly* by Storer & Tevis that grizzly bears had killed a lot of people before they were exterminated from California in 1926. So I still had no reason to doubt that grizzlies were demonic. Three decades passed before I had enough first-hand experience with grizzlies to recognize their capacities for affection and friendship. I also learned that no black bear had ever killed a person in California. Unfortunately, a killing finally did occur in 2023.

Meanwhile, my daydreams of emulating Adams, both as a hunter and friend of grizzly bears, seemed all the more feasible in 1963 when my family moved from Modesto to Concord, at the base of California's Mt. Diablo. That was one of Adams' favorite hunting grounds. By then, grizzlies had been gone for several decades. Yet when I hiked those slopes, where cougars still roamed and occasionally stalked humans, I could imagine myself walking where Adams and the grizzlies had walked, collecting and sometimes sampling the same nuts and fruits which they had eaten, while ever wary of a possible attack.

Over the decades that followed, I turned my daydreams into reality by becoming a wildlife biologist, having thousands of close encounters with wild bears, and befriending a few of them. That might never have happened without the inspiration provided by the real Grizzly Adams.

Adam's life inspired *The Life and Times of Grizzly Adams* movie (1974) and TV show (1977-78), starring actor Dan Haggerty. By a strange quirk of fate, I met Haggerty years later when he and a producer were scouting locations for producing a second Grizzly Adams movie. After seeing clips of my video footage with Alaskan grizzlies, Haggerty and his producer asked whether I'd be interested in participating in the movie, playing the role of Adams as a young man, an idea which amused me to no end, since I did for real with wild bears what they only pretended to do with tame ones. For better or worse, Haggerty passed on to his final award ceremony in the sky before the new movie project got underway.

My transition from just daydreaming about encountering grizzly bears, to actually doing so, began in the summer of 1966, after completing my sophomore year of college with a major in biology. A couple of days before the US Forest Service research team was scheduled to leave for Montana, one of the techs was killed in an auto accident. They needed a replacement but had no time to hire one through normal channels. The job required only a basic knowledge of biology and chemistry, as well as experience in back country hiking and camping. One team member, a friend of my parents, knew that I met those qualifications. He asked whether I could cancel all my summer plans and join them for a few months in the Rocky Mountains. I didn't hesitate. The majesty of glacier-sculpted peaks was irresistible, and the area was supposedly well-populated with bears and other wildlife.

Our research crew was headquartered at Dagger Peak Lodge, several miles south of Darby, Montana. It was owned by a family that I'll refer to as Hutchins. That was on the eastern slope of the Bitterroot Range, which forms the border of Montana and Idaho. Half a century afterward, I recall few details about the lodge except that its

STEPHEN F. STRINGHAM, PHD

buildings were single-story log structures. The Hutchins family lived in one large cabin. Guests, including our crew, occupied small cabins, and our research lab was set up in what would have been the common room where tourists dined and socialized. Beside the lodge was a pasture of roughly two acres, with short sparse grass, a horse-breaking corral, and a barn. A least three horses grazed in the pasture, accompanied by a young bull elk which the Hutchins family had raised from infancy when it was orphaned.

3.2: Hand reared young elk in the ranch meadow.

Throughout the summer of 1966, I assisted in assessing ecosystem impacts by a pesticide designed to eradicate spruce budworm. Those worms were destroying millions of dollars in conifer timber each year. Six days a week, we cruised the surrounding mountains which were thickly forested with spruce, pine and other conifers, as well as aspen and other hardwood. We set out a variety of traps designed to capture insects and small mammals. Periodically we returned and emptied specimens from our traps. By comparing the abundance and variety of insects and small mammals in areas that were treated with the pesticide against areas that weren't treated, we could assess the pesticide's effectiveness in killing budworms, as well as collateral damage to other components of the ecosystem. Back in the lab, other Forest Service technicians and several women hired from local farms sorted and counted the specimens.

On my one free day per week, I either went to town for R&R, or I looked for wildlife. Although it was common to see a black bear skirting our pasture through the trees, I wasn't satisfied with mere glimpses of the shy carnivores. Seeking opportunities to watch bears for hours on end, I hiked into the backcountry. The best place I found was a small valley floored with riparian wetlands. A lazy creek meandered among lush grasses several feet high, among dense stands of willow shrubs. White-barked quaking aspen trees surrounded the wetland, broad leaves audibly rustling in the wind, and seeming to glow as brightly green as fireflies where backlit by the sun. Butterflies and other insects drifted from flower to flower, transferring pollen, or landing by the dozen at muddy spots to get water and perhaps to feast on algae or fungi invisible to my eyes. Whenever the sun was hot, aromatic chemicals evaporated from the conifers, tainting the air with a slight odor like turpentine.

From one hillside I could watch black bears walking belly-deep through the marsh, grazing on the protein-rich sedges grasses, foraging on forbs, digging for roots, or catching trout. Although black bears can be territorial, they commonly share prime feeding sites where food is too abundant to be worth fighting over.

Clouds of mosquitoes and other insects surrounded each bear, sparkling like dust mites in the sunlight. A few times I nervously snuck close to take photos, but at any distance over 50 yards, my 50 mm lens rendered black bears as black dots.

After sneaking in each time, I snuck out again, hoping that the bears would never know I'd been there, lest this make them too wary to be watched again. That precaution was not amiss. After one such session, I looked back to see an adult male stumble on the spot from which I'd been watching. He went berserk with fear and anger for several seconds, pulse-moaning and thrashing nearby bushes as though they were enemies, then burst into a run – unfortunately in my direction, passing within fifty yards of me before disappearing into the forest. By the time I glanced back into the wetland, the other bears which had been grazing there were also gone.

Despite having had several peaceful encounters with black bears, that one berserk reaction to my odor seemed to justify common notions about their aggression and ferocity. My inherent caution was intensified by hearing a radio news story of a girl being mauled by a bear earlier that summer, near Lolo Pass. (That was over 50 years ago, and I recall no details). Although that bear had been tentatively identified as a grizzly, the ID was questioned because there had allegedly been no definite grizzly sightings in the Bitterroots since WWII. Furthermore, I mistakenly assumed that no bear would travel over fifty miles from Lolo to below Darby. So I wasn't overly worried. Granted that I lacked a gun, and pepper spray repellant hadn't yet been invented, but I naively thought I was safe enough by remaining wary. *Fools frolic where angels fear to tread.* If five subsequent decades of living with bears have taught me anything, it's that although few bears seek trouble with people, one must always be prepared to cope with the uncommon exceptions.

As the summer of 1966 drew to a close, our Forest Service research team prepared for the long drive back to Berkeley, California. But first, we wanted to spend the Labor Day weekend hiking and fishing. The owner of Dagger Peak Lodge, Ray Hutchins invited us to join him for a jaunt into renowned trout waters in the back country. During winters, Ray toured the country buying furs of mink, fox, and numerous other animals from ranches that raised furbearers commercially. From spring through fall, however, Ray made his living guiding sport fishermen and hunters. His base camp was about fifteen miles deeper into the Bitterroots, at Black Bear Lake. Labor Day weekend was when Ray made his first pack trip of the season, carrying in tents, food, and other supplies and equipment that would be needed when his hunters started arriving in a week or two. We accepted his invitation to come along, hoping to see new country and catch a fine mess of trout.

We'd be making the trip on horseback, so Ray's riding stock had to be gathered up and prepared. None of his horses had been ridden since the previous fall. They'd had ten months off enjoying a lazy life in the pasture and weren't ready to resume earning their living by carrying riders into the mountains. Not without a fight.

Re-breaking the horses was supervised by Ray's son, assisted by a ranch hand. I seem to recall their names as Burt and Jake. Burt was eighteen, two years younger than me. Blond-haired, powerfully built, he was cocky as only a young cowboy can be. He sneered at us "Californicators," claiming that he could outdo any of us at anything. Tough and aggressive, he buffaloed nearly everyone. When Burt invited us to watch him breaking horses, we figured he just wanted an audience while proving that he was really the better man.

Borrowing tamer mounts from another ranch, Burt, Jake, and I herded Ray's own horses into a corral, then closed the gate. After fitting each horse with a bridle and bit, the fun began. Burt had been pouring beer after beer down his throat all morning. I began wondering whether he could stay in the saddle. He was known as a fairly good roper, but today he just couldn't land his loop. Finally, shaking his head in amused despair, Jake lassoed a palomino for Burt.

By now Burt was furious. Taking the free end of the rope from Jake, Burt snubbed it around a vertical man-high post in the center of the corral. As the horse fought against the rope, it began to strangle. Finally, it collapsed to its knees. Jake got a saddle on the horse, and I held the snub until Burt was seated. When Jake swung the gate open, Burt flipped the rope off the palomino's head.

It took a few minutes for circulation to return to the horse's brain and alert the animal that it was free. Lurching to its feet, the horse took off, racing for the nearby forest. Burt whooped and spurred the horse, looking back at us with a sneer that left no doubt about what he thought of his own cowboy prowess.

Unfortunately, he picked the wrong time to show off. The palomino spotted a low-hanging tree limb and headed right for it. The horse passed under it; Burt didn't. The limb took him in the gut and swept him from the saddle as neatly and gently as if he'd been blown off with a cannon ball. Old Man Hutchins ran for his pickup and we ran for Burt. We helped him to his feet. The wind had been knocked out of him. The pain was intense. Fearing internal injuries, Ray and Jake took him to the hospital thirty miles north in Hamilton.

While they were gone, I broke the horses in a much gentler manner taught to me by an Indian friend, Quis-Qui-Nee. He despised the white man's practice of using violence, fear and pain to break horses. When Quis had to dominate a horse to control it, he didn't choke it with a lariat or ride it bucking bronco style in a corral, raking its flank with spurs. Instead, he led the horse into a stream or lake with a soft bottom, where bucking exhausted the horse, and being bucked off didn't even bruise the rider. Quis-Qui-Nee explained that our fingers look like a bear's claws, and we stand like an upright bear. Worse, when someone mounts a horse, the horse tends to react as though the person is a bear or cougar. Those are the only animals in nature that land on a horse's back, and only in the act of predation. So the first impression we make on horses is that we are predators. This fear needs to be dispelled while you personally bond with each horse – an approach later made famous by another "horse-whisperer" Monte Roberts.

Riding one of the tamer cow ponies, I tried driving each of the rough stock into the creek, one at a time. So long as I sought to control my gelding, I was hopelessly inept at the task. But when I relaxed and let my gelding run the show, he proved his skill as a cutting horse, as he drove each of the wilder horses to the creek. I had the privilege of watching – and riding – a master at work. Once a target horse was in the creek, roping it and slipping on a rope halter was child's play. This was tied to the center of a rope I'd earlier stretched across the stream between trees on opposite banks.

3.3: Stock trucks and our crew. Even my first photo from horseback was blurred by the horse's flinching.

The stream pool was deep enough that each horse's back was at least a foot under water. I slid on and off the horse, putting just a little weight on the animal each time. Even when the horse tried to kick me, it was hampered too much by the water to do me any damage. Finally, when the horse had calmed down, I slid onto its back and sat up. At least a few times, each horse exploded into bucking and I flew off, sometimes turning a front or back flip over its head or rump. Landing in water sure beats landing on rocky ground!

There was no way I could sit a wet bucking horse bareback. But after ten or fifteen minutes of bucking in deep water, each horse was exhausted and quit fighting. Then I rode it around in the river for awhile to be sure the bucking was over before taking it home. Riding bareback might look easy, but straddling a horse's hard backbone is about as comfortable as straddling a fence rail during an earthquake. Ball busting.

When Ray and Bret got back from the hospital, they were amazed to see me riding one of their "wild" horses. When asked how I did it all alone, I just shrugged and said I'd taken them swimming – which being true dyed-in-the-wool cowboys, they were too smart to believe. Rather than try explaining, I left them guessing.

Half-an-hour before dawn on Saturday morning, the other Forest Service biologists and I climbed into our pickups. Ray and Jake drove their red livestock trucks, each big enough to haul several horses. At the trailhead, we loaded the pack horses before mounting our own saddle stock. The sun was just peeking above the horizon when we started the long slow climb into the Bitterroot Wilderness.

I was the only one with a camera, and wondered a bit at Burt's funny grin when he offered me a horse he said was the best one for photographers. This was the same palomino that had dethroned Burt. Not sure what he could be up to, I took him at his word and mounted up. Several miles passed before we caught a glimpse of Dagger Peak, majestically piercing the sky miles ahead.

The scenery was spectacular, demanding to be recorded on film. I stopped the horse to take a picture. Just as I clicked the shutter, the horse flinched, making the camera jerk and ruining my shot. I steadied the animal again and tried once more. Again the horse flinched. This happened each time I prepared to take a shot.

Finally, exasperated, I dismounted and got my picture. Then back onto the horse and up the trail. Again and again, every time I'd try for a shot from horseback, the animal flinched. Having just one roll of 36 frames, I dared not waste any more. I dismounted and finished the trip on foot, walking or jogging, leading the horse.

Shortly after we reached Ray's campsite, about fifteen miles in from the trailhead, he burst out laughing, having such a go at it that he doubled over and nearly choked. "Smartest damned horse I ever saw," Ray gasped. "A person tenses up when he gets ready to snap a picture and the horse flinches. It learned years ago that this gets rid of riders. We always give him to someone with a camera, and it never fails but that they walk most of the trip or forget about taking pictures."

Although I had no way of retaliating against Burt for his nasty trick, I took grim satisfaction recalling how this horse had busted Burt's ribs.

We camped along Black Bear Lake at the base of Dagger Peak, on the eastern slope of the continental divide. The lake's deep cobalt waters are cupped within a glacial cirque – a short, broad U-shaped valley scooped out of the mountain slope by a glacier over hundreds of thousands of years.

3.4: Trapper peak looms in the distance (Adobe Stock).

We arrived in the late afternoon and set up camp, then caught a few trout in the lake. That wasn't enough fish for all the man-hours spent catching them. But not to worry. A mile or few away was a much smaller lake which Ray promised had some of the finest fishing in the Rockies. Early Sunday morning, as soon as there was enough light to see, we climbed down a steep trail to Dollar Lake, which rested near the lip of a hanging valley.

Ray had been so enthusiastic about this tiny circular lake that I thought he'd been pulling my leg. But sure enough, as soon as we arrived and threw in hooks with worms, each of us got a strike.

Within a few minutes, the shallows were teaming with dozens of trout fighting for bait. Ray told us that these fish nearly starved all summer long, waiting for fly hatches in the fall. The hatch was still a couple of weeks away, and the trout were ravenous.

3.5: Glacier cirque containing Black Bear Lake, with Trapper Peak to the right (Adobe stock).

Unfortunately, they were so ravenous that every worm was attacked by a swarm of fish. Somehow, none of the fish ever got to swallow a worm, just to bite it. So despite frenzied strikes, we didn't catch a single fish before every worm was gone. We were stunned. It was almost beyond belief. A hundred strikes and not one fish caught. Some of the guys began searching under rotting logs for worms or grubs, hoping to find more bait. None of us had brought any lures, believing Ray's claim that worms were the thing to use.

By accident, I let my line with its bare hook drop back into the lake … then nearly lost my rod as a trout swallowed the hook and tried racing away. Had my grip been any looser, I'd have had to dive into the lake and chase after my rod. As I hauled this trout ashore, the other guys came up and asked me how I did it. I told them and they laughed in disbelief. But some fish strike at anything shiny. Alaskan Inupiat natives commonly catch fish on bare hooks while fishing through a hole in sea ice. I tried again and immediately caught another trout. Without a worm, my hook attracted few fish, giving one a chance to swallow the hook. Bingo, and into my creel.

Quickly, not really believing it would work, the other guys whipped out their lines and started catching fish on bare hooks. Within half an hour, we had our legal limit of five trout each, strung on a rope.

After we hiked back to Black Bear Lake, Ray dug out the two-foot square of rusty sheet metal he kept at his hunting camp. We set it across four rocks to serve as our fry pan. Ray plopped down a cube of butter to grease the surface and began laying out trout rolled in corn meal. I don't recall ever tasting better fish.

3.6: Trout frying on piece of sheet metal.

After that scrumptious lunch, I found a sunny spot and fell into a deep siesta that lasted into the early afternoon. I awoke full of energy and hungry for adventure. Like a proverbial bear, I wanted to see what was on the other side of the mountain. One of the other guys and I scaled the peak easily enough. I was climbing for the pleasure of it, but my companion tried to make a race of it, only to discover that I topped out a few minutes ahead of him. Angrily, he turned around and descended the way we had come. I chose to instead take a different route so that I could see a new country. The glacial cirque containing Black Bear Lake had been gouged from the eastern face of Dagger Peak. According to our topo map, there was another cirque on a more northerly face of the mountain. I planned to circle around, and descend the northern cirque to that valley floor before returning to camp. My return route would cover at least two miles horizontally after I had descended at least a thousand feet vertically.

3.7: A nanny and kid that I photographed in Glacier National Park years later.

Partway down, I stopped to water a small pine. Hearing a noise behind me, I turned and saw a nanny goat and her kid on a ledge ten feet below. With a couple of bounds, the nanny and kid were on my ledge. The nanny walked towards me, lowering her head, and pointing her horns at me. Her message was clear. "Out of my way!" A fellow biologist studying goats was injured when one of them hooked him and threw him off a cliff. Sharing that fate here would have plunged me hundreds of feet to my death. I had no intention of letting that happen. But I had nowhere to go except back two body-lengths where I held on to a dwarf pine to keep from falling off the ledge which had narrowed to six inches.

Luckily, the nanny and kid weren't interested in me, but in my urine. They ate the soil I'd peed on and nibbled bark from the pine which I'd splashed. Realizing that they were just getting salt, I relaxed and snapped a few photos. Getting closeups that day didn't require a telephoto. They were just yards away. I was in a spot where I couldn't climb up or down the slope around them, so I just had to be patient until they left spontaneously.

Finally, as an alpine glow began to fill the sky above the setting sun, the nanny and kid took off up the cliff, leaving me to resume my descent undisturbed.

That delay with the goats wouldn't have been any problem during midday; but then, towards dusk, it could have been lethal. I still had hundreds of feet of treacherous descent ahead of me before reaching the talus slope, and a hundred more feet of sloping loose rock and boulders. The light was fading, snow flakes were drifting by, and the wind was picking up. Once again, I'd gotten myself into a dicey situation.

There was barely enough light left to see by the time I reached the talus slope, which continued down to a meadow. That slope included boulders the size of houses, separated by crevasses. Falling into a crevasse even ten to twenty feet deep could easily break bones, leaving me stranded to die where I'd never be found. I dared go no farther for several hours until the moon came up, providing barely enough light to distinguish the black crevasses separating boulders from the boulders themselves, which were now covered with a thin dust of snow.

A couple of hours of careful climbing brought me to the bottom of the talus, where the large meadow separated me from a shallow lake. The shortest route back toward camp would have been walking across the meadow. But the ground was soggy, and I didn't relish slogging through mud. To avoid that, I stayed on the dry ground along the rim of the meadow, at the base of the talus. By moving around this lake and across the ridge beyond it, I'd expected to find myself back in the cirque containing Black Bear Lake.

I'd gotten about halfway through the meadow when I ran into a black bear. I'd seen a dark shadow ahead of me that had seemed to be moving but dismissed it as an optical illusion, caused by shifting moonlight as clouds drifted across the sky. When I got to within ten feet, however, a coal-black bear rose from its bed under an overhanging boulder and scurried away deeper into a crevasse.

The adjacent wet meadow provided prime foraging for bears, so I was not surprised that one would be bedded nearby. But I was surprised that it had waited so long to move. Normally, black bears flee when a person is within a few hundred yards. Braver bears usually get shot by hunters. I was puzzled why this bear had been so reluctant to leave its lair.

A few hundred yards farther along the way, I encountered another black bear. Initially, I thought that the first one had circled around ahead of me and lain in wait. But as I got close enough to see this shadowy animal, it was obviously much smaller than the first.

Now I really began to worry. This one might be a yearling and still in the company of its mother. I'd read stories about people being attacked when they got between a cub and its mother (which turns out to be true if it's a grizzly, but almost never if it's a black bear; anyway, this was probably a yearling, old enough to be on its own). Reluctantly, I headed away from the talus, into the wet meadow, where I was soon slogging through ankle-deep muck.

Off to one side of me, a couple of hundred yards away, was a shape that seemed slightly darker than the star-studded sky. It could have been a huge boulder or a big moose, bison, or bear. But I couldn't tell which. Sometimes it seemed to move, but I realized that this might just be the effect of moonlight flickering as clouds passed. Frightened and unsure, I continued forward until I felt nearly certain that the shape abreast of me was an animal.

Retreating at a fast walk through the muck, I headed back to the base of the talus slope. The black shape did not follow and I began again to think my imagination was working overtime. Just to be safe though, I stayed close to the big boulders where I might take refuge if it was a bear sizing me up for a midnight snack.

If the shape in the meadow was a bear, it had to be a grizzly. Rocky Mountain black bears just didn't get that big. But how could it be a griz? Not only had grizzlies supposedly been exterminated from that region long since, but I erroneously doubted that black bears would remain once a grizzly arrived.

Alternating between deep fear and feeling foolish for possibly exaggerating the danger, I continued around the lake until I ran into a third black bear. This one was also under an overhang; but instead of leaving its lair, it retreated as far as possible back under the rock wall. Why were these black bears acting so strangely? I could imagine black bears hiding from a grizzly; but why take refuge so close, rather than retreating into the forest? And if the "shadow" wasn't a griz, what could it be? A bison? None in these mountains. A moose? Normally, one wouldn't be out there by itself with a couple of black bears and a person nearby; nor would black bears be hiding from a moose.

About that time, I looked back out into the meadow. The dark shape seemed as close as ever, despite the fact I'd walked at least a mile from where I'd first seen it. But I still couldn't be sure that it wasn't just an optical illusion. Waves of hot and cold pulsed through my body; fear made me feel so weak that I wondered whether I'd be able to escape a grizzly by slipping between or beneath the huge talus boulders like the black bears had done.

Fear briefly diverted my mind into artistic imagery. I saw the bear-like silhouette as a deeper dark against the darkness, like a hole within night itself. I mused, *If darkness reigns where light dies, then what reigns where even night cannot? The Phantom Grizzly.*

Poetic nonsense, of course From there my mind shifted into prayer as I vowed that if this was a grizzly, and it didn't harm me, I would spend the rest of my life trying to protect bears from human onslaughts.

3:8. The crew built a huge bonfire to guide me back to camp (iStock, Credit Andris Barbans).

Another half-hour brought me to the top of the ridge separating this cirque from the one south of it. From there I could see a big fire at our camp. Feeling relief, I wanted to rush headlong toward my companions. But I knew better than to run from a predator. Also, I could trip on the rough ground and be injured. Disciplining myself not to succumb to terror, I continued downhill slowly and carefully.

Descending the final quarter-mile slope towards camp, at least half-an-hour passed with no further sign of the huge dark bruin. Once more, I began to doubt what I'd seen earlier, to think it had all been a figment of my imagination. I turned back to look uphill behind me. There, a hundred yards up the slope above me were the head and shoulders of a grizzly silhouetted against a golden harvest moon. Moments later its jaws opened and a horrible roar pierced the night. Then it was gone.

3.9: I turned and saw a grizzly's head silhouetted against the moon, just before it opened its jaws and roared angrily (illustration).

So terrified that I nearly soiled myself, I stood petrified, expecting the bear to lunge out of the darkness at any moment. But minute after minute passed with no further sign of the griz. Finally, I calmed down and resumed my walk toward camp. Arriving, I was greeted by a worried crew. They'd been afraid that I was dead or too injured to travel but had built a bonfire to guide me in if I was still mobile. I received a lecture about always carrying matches, a map and a compass even on short day hikes.

When I mentioned the grizzly, Hutchins just laughed. "No griz in these mountains anymore. You've just got a vivid imagination kid." I tried to explain, but the crew laughed me down, even though they knew about the girl being mauled by an alleged grizzly at Lolo Pass.

Ridicule was their attitude in the evening. Not in the morning. We awoke to find that the horses had pulled their picket pins and were gone. Light snowfall left a surface on which the hoof prints were clear. We tracked the horses into the timber a few miles away where they were bunched up. Normally, only a puma, a grizzly, or a very aggressive black bear could have spooked horses so badly.

Ray began to wonder whether maybe I really had seen a griz. Sure enough, after casting around for spoor, we finally found huge bear tracks. Claw tips hit the snow three full inches in front of the finger pads. Grizzly. The animal had circled camp during the night, allowing the horses to catch its scent.

Ray recognized the tracks, even though they were faint on hard ground, and blurred in snowy or muddy spots. Their enormous size was enough to identify it as a large adult male, apparently, one he knew well. Grizzlies of any age and sex were exceedingly rare in Bitterroot Mountains back then in 1966, and Ray had seen tracks of only one adult male, so he figured it was the same one. He had spent his life tracking game, so I didn't dispute him.

It had been five years since he had last seen grizzly tracks near Black Bear Lake. His memories of the bear were not entirely fond because it had caused him considerable trouble and had thwarted all his efforts to bag it for one of his trophy hunters.

Stocking Ray's hunting camp each year took several trips with his pack string, carrying equipment, grub, booze, and other supplies needed for a couple of months of catering to rich hunters. Ray's crew had dug a deep pit where they cached the items brought on each trip. Only when several pack loads had accumulated did Ray feel it worth leaving a man to set up camp and guard it.

One year (probably around 1960), they'd brought in a bunch of canned goods late in August and buried them in the pit. When they returned a few weeks later, they found the pit had been dug up by a bear. The bruin had bitten a lot of the cans and torn open a few, including those filled with jam and peanut butter. At that time, some of the best jams in North America were produced under the *Empress* label and sold in a 1- or 2-liter tin with a press-on lid. The bear had popped off each lid and had polished off every one of the dozen cans in the stash. And I do mean polished; the inside of each can looked as if it had been burnished by a jeweler. That must have been one happy griz.

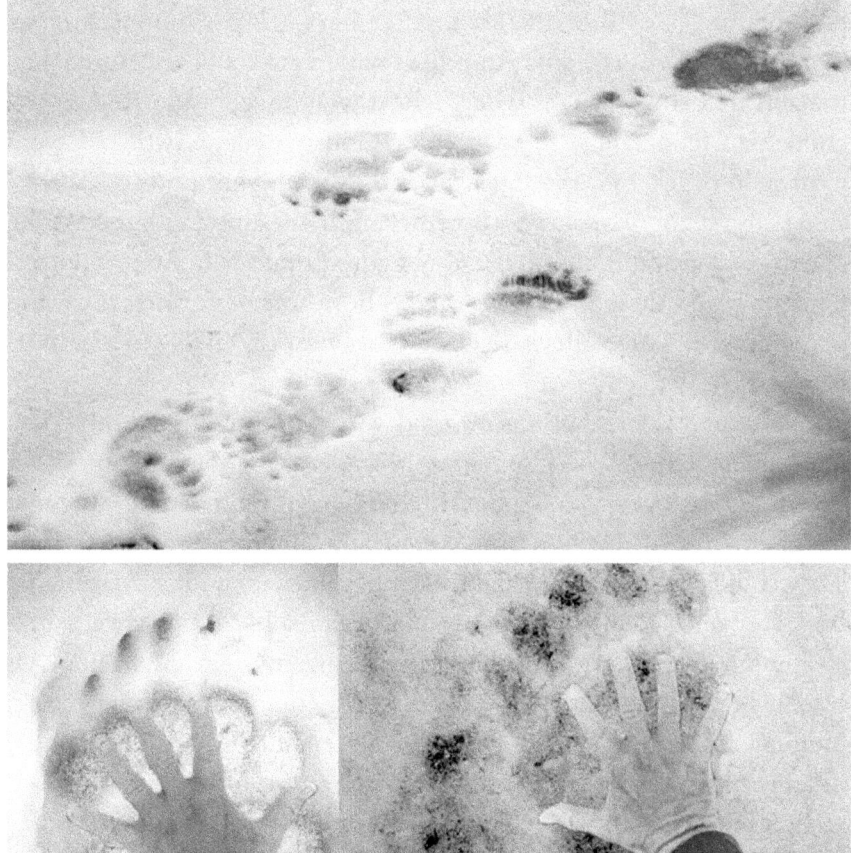

3.10: Grizzly footprints in snow. *top*: tracks going from the lower left corner to the upper right (Adobe stock); *bottom left* handprint (Adobe stock) and *right* footprint (Dreamtime stock).

After several years of not having any more bear problems or seeing any more grizzly tracks, Ray thought the big male had either died or moved on to another territory. Now here it was back again in 1966. Ray would need to take a lot more precautions to protect this year's camp than he'd been taking during the interim.

Prior to this huge boar's disappearance five years earlier, harvesting it had been an obsession with Ray. Now it was again. For years thereafter, he employed every trick he could think of to find the bear or lure it within rifle shot. After harvesting a mountain goat, bighorn, or elk, he used its gut pile as bait to attract bears. He stashed the guts in a grove of trees where a bear would feel it was hidden well enough to feed safely. In reality, Ray and his clients would have a clear field of fire into the lair from a hideout higher on the opposite slope, about 200 yards away. By entering their shooting blind before dawn and leaving it after dark, Ray figured that his hunters wouldn't be spotted by their prey. That high above the bear, with the wind rising up out of the valley, the hunters' scent wasn't likely to reach the bruin.

None of his precautions worked with this huge male, however. Ray adopted the name I suggested, *Phantom Griz*, because he never saw it, just its occasional spoor. Before dawn one morning, Ray and his clients hiked to the ambush spot and quietly began their vigil. They waited all day. Finally, at dusk, they gave up and started hiking back to camp. That's when they made the sobering discovery of a steaming pile of bear dung about fifty feet from their hide. The turds were over 2" in diameter, which could only come from a large grizzly. Judging from the spoor, Ray figured *Phantom* had been there watching him and his clients for a least an hour. Had the bear been so inclined, it could have attacked and mauled all of them before they could defend themselves.

The bear was never shot. Since 1975, all grizzlies south of Canada have been protected as Threatened Species, under the Endangered Species Act. For another decade, until he retired, Ray still occasionally ran across giant tracks.

I reported our sightings to the US Fish & Wildlife Service several years later when I read its official claim that the last griz in the Bitterroots was shot just after WWII. But our sightings were dismissed as unconfirmed – as though a professional bear hunter and a bear biologist couldn't tell a grizzly from a black bear. Apparently, a prolonged lack of grizzlies in the Bitterroots was legally necessary before new grizzlies could be reintroduced – which the USFWS was proposing to do. That was my first, but far from my last, experience butting my head against the stone edifice of politically correct deception by a federal or state natural resource management agency.

Nor was it my last reminder of the added risk of hiking or climbing solo. Sometimes it can't be helped. But ever after, I took the precaution of carrying at least a fanny pack with survival gear. Once bear-grade pepper spray became available a few decades later, I always carried at least one can, and usually two, so that if one ran out or failed, I had a backup. When possible, I've also carried some kind of 2-way radio or phone.

Hunting for bears near a gut pile was a well-established practice even a century ago, as described by Wm. H. Wright in his 1909 book *The Grizzly*, the first book ever written about these bears in North America. Nevertheless, it is a hazardous practice. Some bears are so attuned to hunters that they allegedly stalk hunters, waiting for one to kill an elk or moose. Ungulate (= hoofstock) hunters commonly claim that grizzlies are attracted by gun shots and come running, expecting to claim a feast. However, I've never heard a bear hunter claim to have attracted bears by firing a gun instead of using food bait; and I have doubts about grizzlies patiently following hunters around in hopes of being fed.

Yet, I have little doubt that bears do come running when they detect the scents of rumen (stomach) contents and perhaps of blood.

STEPHEN F. STRINGHAM, PHD

Depending on a grizzly's boldness, it might quickly rush in to claim the whole carcass; or it might wait until the carcass has been gutted and the meat removed. Numerous hunters have been attacked by a grizzly that tried to usurp their ungulate carcass. Sometimes the person was injured or killed; in other cases, it was the bear that died; or both.

3.11: "Watch your back Jack!" After killing a big game animal, keeping an eye out for bears is critical (Artistic recreation from a Ron Aldrich photo).

Why a hunter is suddenly attacked in that situation isn't entirely clear. When one bear is feeding on the carcass of an ungulate, sea lion or whale, a second bear attracted to the carcass doesn't typically rush in and attack the first bear. More commonly, the new arrival approaches slowly, perhaps circling around the carcass, perhaps to identify the first bear and to reveal its own identity and social rank. If the first bear is perceived as higher-ranking, the second bear might wait until the first bear is finished before attempting to feed. Or the second bear might make hesitant approaches with submissive body language to test whether it will be allowed to feed there too. Alternately, if the new arrival perceives the first bear as lower-ranking, it's likely to walk or rush forward, allowing the first bear time to flee without being attacked. After the first bear has thus acknowledged its lower rank, it is sometimes allowed to return and resume feeding near the dominant individual. This is similar to the way two bears interact when competing for a prime fishing site on a salmon stream. Non-violent displacement of subordinate individuals is far more common than attack. I know of no reason why a bear would be much more likely to just attack a hunter beside his kill unless the bear has signaled the hunter to move away, but the hunter was oblivious, whereupon the frustrated bear became violent. Anyone near the carcass of a large animal should remain constantly wary enough to detect any approaching bear before it attacks.

Although a grizzly will sometimes share a large carcass with another grizzly, I've heard of few cases where a grizzly was content to share with one or more wolves, and vice versa. And bears typically don't share prey carcasses with humans. Whereas a hunter might gladly accept any share of a bear's fresh kill that the bear would allow, rarely does anyone have any interest in sharing or usurping a rotting ungulate carcass. So a bear gains nothing by threatening or attacking a passerby. Unfortunately, not all bears know that. There are numerous cases where a carcass-defending grizzly has attacked or tried to attack someone who just chanced to be walking or boating past – as happened in 1995, when Marcie Trent, 77 and her 45-year-old son Larry Waldron hiked down the McHugh Creek Trail, near Anchorage, Alaska. Once someone is killed, they too become meat from a bear's perspective.

* * *

A few years after the deaths on McHugh Creek, I was living north of Anchorage, where the small community of Wasilla butts up against the Chugach Mountains. A moose died in a wooded area about 100 yards from my home and about ten yards from a school bus stop. After a neighbor noticed the foul odor and informed me, I grabbed a shotgun and investigated, prepared in case it was defended by a bear. Not yet. Returning home, I printed signs and posted them on the road for more than 100 yards in each direction, warning pedestrians to walk on the opposite side of the road and to keep watch for any bears. Then I stood guard as school buses arrived and disgorged students. Elementary school children generally took my advice. High school students, however, tended to ignore it and actually walked over to look at the carcass – where they would have been defenseless if a bear had been present. I phoned the Fish & Game department, requesting that they remove the carcass, only to learn that coping with carcasses had to be handled by the public. Before nightfall, we rented a backhoe and buried the carcass, after covering it with caustic lime, then wetting the dirt above it with bleach. The unwillingness of the high school students to take precautions was a sobering reminder of how much bear-human conflict results from some people who expect wildlife to behave according to human rules and preferences. Now and then, such people win a Darwin Award (extinction).

When Grizzlies Get High

Glacier National Park, September 1966

When the Forest Service crew left Dagger Peak Lodge and drove directly back to California, I detoured north a few hundred miles to Glacier National Park, hoping to see grizzlies. All campgrounds were full on the Park's west side, but I was able to reserve a site on the east side. Logan Pass was already closed by snow, so I drove the long way around. After following Highway 2 from the town of West Glacier eastwards to the Blackfeet Indian Reservation (where I later lived and taught college), I turned north at East Glacier Park along the incredibly beautiful *Looking Glass Valley* road, then continued along a winding two-lane highway to St. Mary's Lake. From there, *Going to the Sun Highway* led me to a campground surrounded by one of the most spectacular vistas in America.

Rising almost vertically on each side of St. Mary's Lake are glacier-carved walls thousands of feet high, topped by peaks as jagged as a wolf's jaw. All afternoon, those peaks had been wrapped by heavy dark clouds that were forming nowhere else. Thousands of feet above me, the clouds writhed in the wind like living things. Finally, toward evening, those winds became strong enough to shred the puffy clouds into long thin cirrus veils, as though glowing red hair snarls were being brushed into free-flowing tresses. Left behind by the clouds were glistening stone walls, most as dark as obsidian or Blackfeet pipestone. Yet one scarlet sedimentary layer turned blood red in the brilliant clear light of the setting sun.

3.12: St. Mary's Lake at sunset (Adobe stock image).

Fortunately, this was a glory that I didn't have to enjoy alone. After an entire summer without a date, I had just met Carrie. A lithe girl with a pale pinched face, her white-blond hair hung straight from her braided leather headband to her wasp-narrow waist. Complementing her ankle-length velveteen dress of deepest purple was a belt of silver Navaho conchos, inlaid with turquoise and red coral. Attractive though the outfit was, it would have marked her as a "wanna-be" – wanna-be Indian – at the Labor Day "Blackfeet Indian Days" powwow that she and her friends had just attended. Although some of the Indians would have snickered, that wouldn't have stopped the young bucks from courting her. But for now, she was mine.

As dusk filled the valley, we strolled to the lake shore, then back to the campground. In the couple of hours we'd known one another, Carrie and I had become thoroughly enchanted – laughing quietly as we walked, shoulders touching tentatively at first, but soon rubbing together like lonesome cats, purring. Her warm scent of Patchouli oil was intoxicating.

She and several friends had the campsite next to mine. They were traveling, packed like cigarettes in an old Volkswagen van whose factory paint job was buried several layers deep in peace signs, love symbols, and other Hippie graffiti, except where rust had eaten holes through the fenders.

Accepting their invitation to dinner, I got my first introduction to brown rice, tofu, and tabbouleh. It was a big change from my normal meat and 'tatters diet, but not bad, not bad at all. And the company was grand.

After dinner, everyone grabbed a beer and kicked back around the campfire. Guitars, mouth harps, and kazoos appeared. Carrie's pleasant voice graced the songs of Joan Baez as smoke curled upwards from joints passed 'round the circle. Already high on infatuation, I needed no chemical assistance. I just mimed an occasional sip and drag. That sufficed to keep my hosts mellow until the deepening chill of night convinced most of them it was time to sack out.

Not wanting to separate, Carrie and I remained by the fire, huddled together under a ragged quilt, faces toasting like marshmallows as we traded tentative kisses. Our warming hormones might have soon boiled over had we not been interrupted.

A black bear wandered into camp. Expecting my sweet lady to be scared, I prepared to play the big brave man by shooing the hairy panhandler away. But Carrie sensed no danger. She opened the leather pouch at her waist and pulled out several cubes of raw brown sugar. After tossing several to the bear, she smiled coyly, popped a cube into her own mouth, then asked if I wanted one too.

"Thanks, but I don't like sugar," I declined.

"Not the sugar dummy," Carrie smiled, "the acid." Then I understood. The cubes were laced with LSD.

The bear was now just a body length away as it searched for more goodies until my sudden leap up spooked it into loping off into the night. "Are you insane?" I yelled. "Feeding acid to a bear is the craziest stunt I've ever heard of. If that bear freaks out, it could kill someone!"

So much for our budding romance. Scornfully, Carrie chided me, "Just because you're an uptight asshole doesn't mean I have to be. It's fun to get stoned, and I'll bet the bears like tripping too." Fuming, she stormed away.

I don't know whether any of the bears *tripped out* that night, much less *freaked out*. But if so, they did it away from the campground and no one was hurt. But what about the following summer when two young women were killed during the night of 13 August? The best reference on bear maulings is Dr. Steve Herrero's popular and informative book *Bear Attacks*. He explains how bears come to associate food with people, and thus to seek food where they find people, especially at camping sites where cooking has occurred and food is stored. Once a bear is close to a person, looking for food, it might start viewing people as potential prey. Or if someone tried scaring it away, the bear might attack in perceived self-defense. Both of the 1967 victims were young women who had been sleeping near sources of anthropogenic food, and thus at high risk of a bear encounter.

Had the attacks occurred on widely separated nights, those factors might fully explain the tragedies. However, the fact that these were the first killings within Glacier Park and that two bears became killers during the same night, over nine miles apart – the only incident of its kind ever recorded – suggests that some other common factor aggravated the maulings. No such factor has ever been identified, and the possibility is normally swept aside. However, my experience with Carrie made me suspect that drugs were involved. Although the killers were two different grizzlies separated by miles of mountain terrain, a person in good condition or a bear could have walked that distance between morning and night. Or a person driving through the Park might have left sugar cubs for bears at more than one location.

But even if drugs were partly responsible for these fatalities, the bears would not have been near the people when they became homicidally predatory had they not become accustomed to foraging near people for garbage and unsecured groceries.

Attacks cannot occur unless bears encounter people. So the firewall of most bear safety programs is keeping people separate from bears. This is easiest if people don't seek bears (e.g. to view or hunt them), bears don't seek foods that are near people, and if bears don't react to people as sources of food, much less as food. This isn't to say that people can't peacefully coexist with bears, even while watching them at distances of 100 yards or less, as I have done countless times since them. But that works only where food is normally abundant, and several other conditions are met, which isn't typical of most bear habitats.

Multimedia for Chapter 3.

4

ALIEN ABDUCTIONS

The foregoing chapters focused on portraying the typical behavior of bears during close encounters, in stark contrast to popular tales of the occasional encounters where a bear injured or killed someone. But traumatic bear-human interactions are not limited to what bears do to humans. They also include traumas inflicted by humans on bears. Nothing more needs to be said about the physical and emotional traumas suffered by bears when they are hunted or harassed. But it is important to acknowledge how we have sometimes harmed bears without intending to, either through insensitivity or ignorance.

We've all heard stories of someone being abducted, immobilized and subjected to weird medical examinations by aliens. If bears could talk, they'd probably tell similar tales about being captured, immobilized, and examined by wildlife biologists. Although we put considerable effort into minimizing trauma, a lot of trial and error has been required for us to find ways of better achieving that goal. Furthermore, our standards of minimal trauma have risen since we began handling bears half-a-century ago. As bearanoia and demonizing bears have declined, and as our understanding of them increased, so too has our concern for their welfare. Especially biologists like myself, who observe bears at close range, want bears to be comfortable with our presence. That is most feasible if we assure that any time we handle them, we treat them with standards approaching how we would handle a fellow human. This chapter recalls events and adventures during this decades-long transition.

Barrels of Bears

4.1a: Redwood forest (Getty Images).

Although I eventually became a wildlife biologist, specializing in bears, that was not until 1969, after completing my Junior, Senior, and Post-Senior years majoring in Biological Oceanography (Marine Ecology) at Humboldt State University, in northern California. Lying on the coast, just south of the Oregon border, Humboldt County has long been a center for logging and commercial fishing. The University had strong programs in several branches of the natural resource field, including wildlife management.

During the summer after I completed my BSc degree, I ended up sharing a house with Kelly and Jasper, two wildlife management grad students under Professor Archie Mossman, a mutual friend. Jasper studied waterfowl; Kelly studied black bears. When I told Kelly about my experiences with bears in Montana, he asked whether I wanted to volunteer as his unpaid assistant. It was another offer I couldn't refuse.

4.1b: Visiting my old haunts in 2013. Most of the forest where I worked in the 1960's had been logged, including areas that were incorporated into the national park. But what remained was still a delight to explore.

Lying just a few miles inland from the Pacific Ocean, this was redwood country, with trees towering up to 350 feet into the air. Most mornings, fog rolling in from the ocean filled and chilled the forest. Noon passed before the fog burned off and the forest became hot and muggy, with shafts of sunlight lasering down through the arboreal gloom, bathing the trees and ferns in patches of light. Where the redwoods were tightly packed together, each tree's canopy of needle-covered branches shaded the forest floor so heavily that the plant understory was mainly ferns. By contrast, where some of those giants had fallen, or where the land opened into swamp or meadow, the understory was so dense with brush that it was almost impenetrable by humans. Nevertheless, it was a great habitat for bears – currently just black bears, but at one time also for grizzlies.

Virtually anywhere that black bears coexist with humans, conflicts occur. Bears are attracted to many human-source (i.e., anthropogenic) foods, including agricultural crops, garbage, or feed for birds, pets and livestock. Bears are also highly curious and powerful. This leads them to investigate buildings, farm yards and other areas where they can do extensive damage. The quick and dirty solution to ending a bear's depredations is to kill it. Sport hunters also want to kill bears. Achieving a balance between killing enough bears to limit depredations and satisfy sport hunters, without killing so many that the health of the bear population is jeopardized, is the responsibility of each state's Fish & Game department. Expert management of a bear population requires information about the abundance and distribution of bears in each region of each state. It also requires information on their birth and death rates. Birth rates are governed by food supply. Death can come from bears being purposefully killed or as an inadvertent byproduct of mining, logging, road construction and numerous other human activities.

Until recently, bears had been killed willy-nilly as vermin with little restraint. However, as that devastated one bear population after another, conservationists called a halt by having bears reclassified as big game animals, and demanding that their populations be managed scientifically. This endeavor was pioneered in the early 1960s on grizzlies by John and Frank Craighead at Yellowstone National Park, and on black bears by Al Erickson in Michigan, Lynn Rogers in Minnesota, and Chuck Jonkel in Montana. Kelly's study attempted to do the same thing on the northern California coast.

4.2a: Barrel trap.

4.2b: Culvert trap (Ann Bryant photo).

Obtaining essential information requires identifying some individuals in the population and following their fates over a number of years. This was done by capturing, measuring, marking and monitoring the animals. Kelly planned to capture bears in barrel traps. Each trap was made out of two or three 55-gallon barrels welded end to end, with the intervening lids cut off, forming a single chamber roughly eight to twelve feet long. Another trap was made from a similar length of steel culvert about three feet in diameter. Barrel traps were light enough to be transported in a pickup; each culvert trap was so heavy that it was mounted on a trailer.

For bait, we used road-kill deer carcasses, rotting fish from the Eureka wharf, and any other foul meat we could find. The worse it smelled, the better it attracted bears. This was placed at the far end of the trap, attached to a trigger. Once a bear had crawled in far enough to reach the bait and yank the trigger, its feet were well inside and safe from injury when the trap's guillotine-style sliding door slammed down.

Each trap was placed near a road, in hopes of catching a bear overnight, although it sometimes took a week or more before a given trap was successful. Overall, we didn't capture more than one or two bears a week. Just as well, since the experience terrified and infuriated some bears.

We were constantly worried that a trapped bear would be discovered by a passer-by who might be injured trying to release the bear or to touch or harass it through the 2"x2" windows we'd cut into the metal barrel or culvert. Or someone might stick something through one of these little windows and injure the bear. Even if no one bothered the bear, being stuck in a trap during the heat of the day could badly stress the animal. Such hazards had to be minimized.

We thus baited each trap only in the early evening, then returned after dawn the following day to see what we'd caught. Some bears detected us coming before we got within a few hundred yards, then panicked, trying to escape, bellowing, roaring, and pulse-moaning, so furiously that we were terrified many times, only half-believing that no bear could break out. Other bears remained quiet, cowering in the trap, as though hoping to remain undetected, as we drew near. When one of us peeked in through a tiny window, however, the bear was likely to lunge across those few feet of space and slam both forepaws against the metal wall of the trap, creating a horrendous racket. For better or worse, we caught few bears that summer. Most of my experience capturing bears was gained later, in Montana.

Rocky Mountain Bears

Kelly's project was just one of hundreds of investigations inspired by the pioneering studies of Lynn Rogers, Charles Jonkel, and the Craighead team. Back then, in the late 1960s, John and Frank Craighead were professors at the University of Montana and at the State University of New York, respectively. Their research was done on grizzly bears in and around Yellowstone National Park starting in 1959. Lynn and Chuck, by contrast, were doctoral students. Lynn worked under Al Erickson in Michigan; Chuck studied under Ian McTaggart Cowan at the University of British Columbia. Chuck's study focused on black bears just west of Glacier National Park, near the Canadian border. After finishing his Ph.D., Chuck turned to research on polar bears for several years, before returning to Montana where he too became a professor at the University of Montana in Missoula. He not only resumed research on the west side of Glacier National Park but fostered projects all along the Canadian Border from the Blackfeet Indian Reservation, on the east side of the Park, westwards thorough Idaho into Washington.

Of all those early pioneers, only Lynn Rogers is still going strong. Starting out just a couple of years before my work with Kelly, Lynn went on to become recognized as one of the world's premier carnivore biologists. Whereas the Craigheads are best known for their research, and Jonkel for his activism, Rogers is well known for both.

* * *

While working with Kelly back in 1969, I could never have dreamed of one day having the privilege of working with any of these pioneers. Indeed, I was never a formal student of any of them. But we did develop informal relationships that shaped my development as a bear biologist. In the 1970s I spent much of one summer working for Chuck as a volunteer field assistant. In the 1990s, we interacted frequently to help integrate western scientific approaches to grizzly conservation with the traditional cultures of both Salish-Kootenai and Blackfeet Indian Nations.

Back in the 1970s, Chuck's beard and hair hadn't yet begun resembling the snowy peak of a Rocky Mountain massif. His fur was just beginning the grey, and the grandfatherly manner for which he eventually became so beloved was still merely paternal. Yet he picked up stray grad students like some people pick up stray dogs. He also picked up useable furniture and other items discarded on roadsides or in a landfill, which he rightly expected would be treasured by some impoverished students. He was one of the most caring men I have ever known, not only about humanity, wildlife, and wildlands in general, in the abstract; but also about individuals. He cared about the welfare of students whether they were formally assigned to him by the University, or merely wandered in, gravitated to his projects and offered to work like slaves just for the privilege of helping to "make a difference." I was one of those strays, albeit for just half of the summer of 1976. He accepted my offer of free help, in exchange for learning the tricks of the trade.

Capturing Bears

To join Chuck's bear crew, I drove from Missoula north to Polebridge, Montana on the western side of Glacier National Park, and then west to the cabin that the crew used as their headquarters. Among the crew were Mike Madel, Pete Zager, Chris Servheen, and Jamie Jonkel, Chuck's son – all of whom went on to become highly renown in the world of bear research and conservation.

4.3: When a bear bit into the mesh covering the back of the barrel trap, gaps between the strands couldn't be much larger than 1", as shown here, to prevent the bear from breaking a canine tooth (Courtesy BearSmart.com).

The cabin was already packed with students. No room for one more. I lived in the back of my pickup, which I covered with a junked camper shell that I found discarded at a land fill. Laying boards from side to side on the upper rims of the pickup bed, I created a platform for my sleeping pad and bag, with storage underneath. A board running lengthwise on the passenger side of the pickup back served as my dining table and desk. A board on the other side was used for preparing meals on a 3-burner Coleman camp stove fueled with white gas. Running an electric cord from the truck's battery into the camper shell, I attached a 12 V brake light bulb, and voila! Plenty of electric light to work and read by. A propane stove provided sufficient warmth on cold nights. Ventilation was more than adequate.

I was soon back helping to capture bears – this time both blackies and grizzlies. We still used a barrel trap or culvert trap when capturing a bear where some bystander might get close to the trapped bear, to minimize the risk of the person being hurt or harming the bear.

4.4a: We waited until each bear was unconscious before pulling it out of the trap. Later, when we were done, we returned it to the trap where it could recover safely.

4.4b: Before we released it back into the wilds (Courtesy BearSmart.com).

We used 1x1" heavy gauge metal "screening" at the end of the trap. That mesh was necessary for ventilation and so that we could see inside and view the bear or bears, in case we caught a mother with cubs or a pair of siblings. However, in their attempts to escape or attack, some bears shoved their lower jaw through one of the inch-wide gaps, trying to bite and rip the metal. One bear broke a lower canine. To prevent more injuries, we welded smaller mesh across the opening so that a bear couldn't get its teeth caught there.

4.5a: Leg-hold traps. Traps built for grizzly bears are powerful enough to snap a leg bone (illustration).

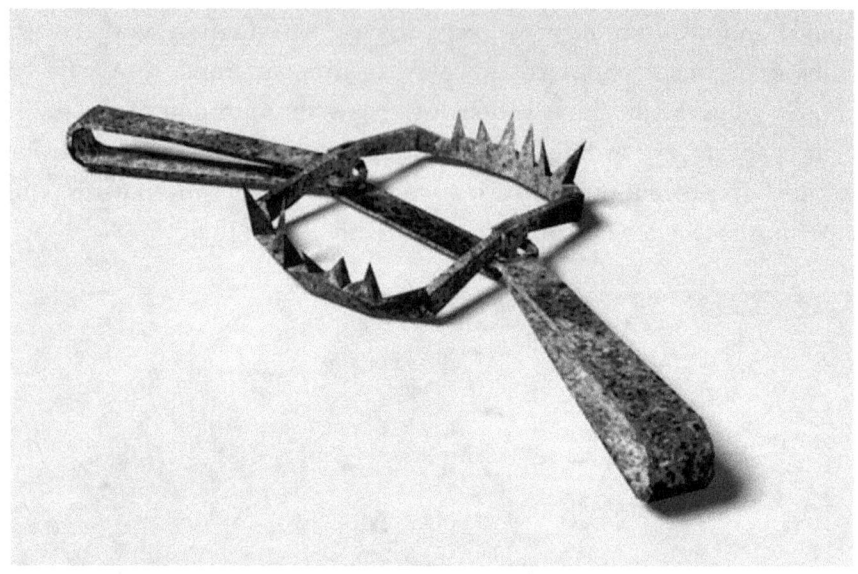

4.5b: Traps built for grizzly bears are powerful enough to snap a leg bone (illustration).

4.5c: The jaws of some traps were rimmed with sharp teeth that could slice through muscles and tendons, crippling a bear, and preventing it from pulling free (Dreamstime image).

While I stayed at the mesh near the bear's head, to keep it distracted, one of the other guys moved to a window behind the bear's rump. He inserted a pole with a syringe on the end, filled with a knock-out drug. This was jabbed into the bear's rump, and after about fifteen minutes, the bear passed out for an hour or so.

After pulling a bear out, we attached colored plastic flags to its ears and a colorful marine rope collar to its neck, from which hung a plastic ID tag of the kind cattle wore in their ears. Any time one of these bears was spotted during the coming months or years, its collar and ear tags would reveal its identity. Repeated re-sightings would indicate where each bear spent most of its time, and how it used its habitat.

In remote locations, where no one was likely to stumble on a bear trap, we preferred leg-hold traps. These were *not* the historical jaw traps designed to injure an animal so badly it could not escape, holding it until it could be killed. Those had a pair of sharp-toothed jaws that snapped closed around a bear's hand or foot so powerfully that they severed muscles and tendons and sometimes broke bones. Traps designed for large grizzly bears could weigh over 100 pounds. However, those are expensive and hard to haul around. Nowadays, even lethal trapping is usually done with a cable snare, much like the ones which we use when capturing a bear for research purposes.

When trapping bears that we wanted unharmed, we used Aldrich Foot Snares. Each snare was made of heavy-duty aircraft-quality stainless steel cable, ranging in thickness from a quarter inch for black bears to three-eighths inch or more for grizzlies. One end of the cable was looped around the trunk of a tree, then locked in place with cable clamps. The other end of the cable was also looped. But this loop moved freely so that it could close down on the foot of an unwary bear. The two halves of the cable were joined in the center with a swivel so that no matter how much a bear twisted around, it couldn't kink and fray the cable – the main cause of cable breakage.

Before laying the free loop flat, usually level with the ground, I dug a small pit up to six inches deep, using a garden trowel. The dirt removed was scooped into a canvas bag and later emptied some distance away. In the pit, I positioned a trigger and set the spring. When a bear stepped through the loop, onto the trigger, the spring would snap the loop closed around the wrist or ankle of the bruin. As soon as the bear jerked back, the loop would lock in place. Then, no matter how the bear fought, it couldn't break free.

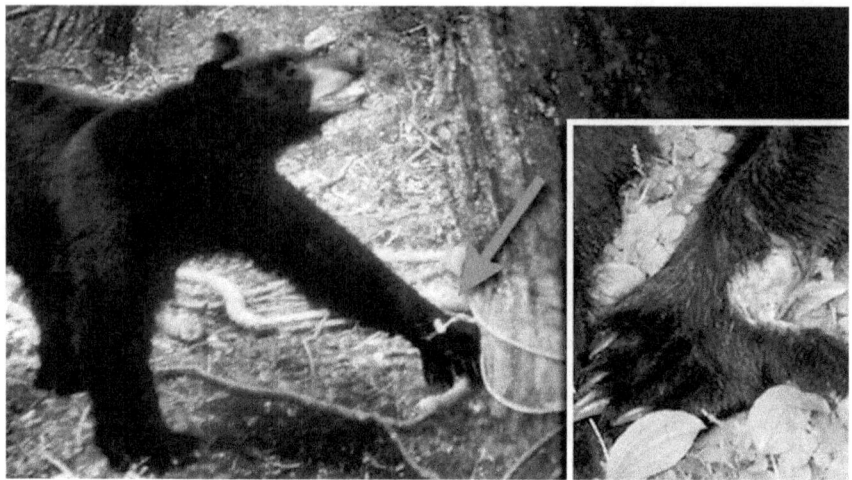

4.6: Cable-inflicted injury to a bear's wrist. Such injuries can usually be prevented if one installs a powerful shock-absorbing spring on the cable (courtesy, Animal Protection League of New Jersey).

We thought that these snares would be safe for bears. But good intentions aren't enough. Despite our precautions, some bears suffered lacerations or strained muscles and tendons. Those problems were reduced, but not entirely eliminated by equipping each snare with a heavy shock absorber. This was made from a second-hand spring of the kind used to keep car hoods up while the engine is being worked on. Normal cars have one such spring on each side of the hood. Our first ones were obtained by raiding a junk yard, at 25 cents per spring.

It was one thing to have a trap. It was another thing to get a bear to step into it. That's where *sets* came in. A *set* refers to the way a trapper sets up the surroundings of the trap to hide it and guide the animal into the trap. Our favorite set was a covey – a kind of nook. A covey was made by placing small logs, up to say six inches in diameter and six feet long, in an *A*-shape. The peak of the *A* rested against the trunk of the tree to which the snare was attached.

The largest logs were laid at the base, with progressively smaller ones higher up. A covey made this way was stable enough that it didn't topple over when accidentally bumped by an animal – although they were easily torn apart by an angry or curious bear.

The purpose of the *A*-shape was, of course, to funnel the bear's "hand" exactly where we wanted it – approaching the trap from just the right angle, and making it place its hand inside the snare loop, on top of the trigger. (The bones of a bear's hand are so similar to those of a human hand that I was once nearly arrested for grave robbing after I collected the hand of a dead bear. To prove my innocence, I had to show where I'd found the dead bear).

The cross-bar of the *A* was one or more small logs placed in front of the snare. Bears are reluctant to step on top of small logs, especially those which readily roll underfoot. Instead, a bear will usually step over the obstruction, placing its foot on the ground just beyond. And, *just beyond* is exactly where I placed a snare. I often used the foot-wide leaves of a thimbleberry or cow parsnip plant to cover the loop and trigger. Over the leaf, I sprinkled dirt, humus, conifer needles, and small leaves of various plants. Soon, there was no visible sign of the snare.

Odor was another matter. Some trappers remove or mask any scent of the trap itself or of themselves by boiling the trap, sometimes in a special *soup*. Many trappers develop their own kinds of *soup* and have to be prodded to tell anyone else how they did it. Frankly, most of us didn't worry about having our scent on a trap and still caught bears often enough. Any bear familiar with people learns to associate human odor with strange but tasty snacks, whether as handouts or garbage. Coveys with human odor seemed to work as well as those without.

The most important odor is that of the bait. In the beginning, I used bacon or sardines, which could be smelled a long way off. Sometimes I even carried a propane torch to singe the bait, producing smoke that wafted far and wide on the wind. Those baits worked fairly well, especially on bears that had never been trapped before. But they were prohibitively expensive. The next thing we tried was rotting meat. Every week or so, we'd make the rounds of local stores, visiting meat departments, and collecting up to a hundred pounds of scraps and discards.

A surprising amount of this meat still smelled *okay* and soon found its way down the gullets of *starving* grad students, including yours truly. Except for an occasional trout, that was the only meat I ate all summer. And, except for the times I got sick eating meat that was a trifle too well-aged, the only drawback of this diet, like that of feasting on beans for most meals, was the ease with which every bear within a hundred miles could smell me coming.

Meat baits like that were, however, only for greenhorns like myself. More experienced trappers, such as Chuck's son Jamie, were members of an arcane society older and more secretive than the Masons or the Knights Templar.

Real trappers like those guys sometimes joked about secret *soups* to de-scent a trap, but that was mostly kidding around. *Bait* secrets, however, were deadly serious. To be sure, some baits are much better than others. But I sometimes wondered whether the real importance of secret *baits* is turning the otherwise dull, mundane job of bear trapping into something exciting, just reeking with prestige – as illustrated by a tongue-in-cheek tale which I use for bringing a bit of humor into my lectures.

One day I was hiking along a creek that eventually drained into the North Fork of the Flathead River. I smelled something awful – kind of like I'd expect a putrefying skunk carcass to smell. But, no, it wasn't a dead skunk. Just a live trapper. Around a bend in the trail came a tall lanky figure. His grungy clothes hung in rags. His teeth were rotted to the gums. He hadn't washed since John the Baptist was dunking people in rivers. By the time he was within arm's length, my eyes were watering and I was holding my breath, wishing my nostrils could clamp closed like those of a moose.

Hoping to get past the fellow as quickly as possible, I smiled with closed lips and raised eyebrows, while moving to the right side of the trail to pass. He stepped in front of me. I shifted left. He did too. A couple of more Keystone Kops moves like that, and we were still face to face. The air in my lungs was gone and I had to take a breath. Better that I had suffocated.

With the oxygen came a stench that nauseated me instantly. I fell to my knees and retched.

"Het shore stinks, doan het," said the friendly fellow. Dumbly, miserably, I nodded, while my stomach flip-flopped again. Finally, I turned and looked up at him. He smiled, showing all the black stubs of his teeth above livid red gums. "T'aint me. Sits da bait. Seekrit. Make sit ma self." The sicker I looked, the happier he was.

Trappers like that old cuss are fortunately rare. More conventional trappers take great care to minimize all body odor that would otherwise advertise their presence to bears and other furbearers. Some trappers even avoid aftershave and cologne. Likewise, I've met a number who eschew manufactured bug dope, preferring to make their own out of false hellebore or other plants.

In any event, it is normally not the trappers but their baits that stink. Good baits stink something awful, and super baits would take the starch out of a boardroom of Swizz bankers. Worse, dedicated trappers hoard mason jars of bait with as much zeal as bankers hoard gold.

The only thing trappers would tell me about creating my own bait was to use a combination of odors that both whet a bear's appetite and arouse its curiosity.

The bait which I most wanted to reproduce was that concocted by an old trapper whom I'll call Kurt Eveans. It was said to be so effective that bears, wolves, mountain lions, and other animals came from miles around, just for the privilege of sniffing it – not withstanding the brief and violent end to their curiosity.

Now most trappers at least share recipes with their nearest and dearest. But not old Kurt. So when he finally gave up the ghost quite a number of years ago, he left behind a grieving widow and a suicidally depressed son, Lawrence. As I pieced the story together from snatches of conversation by various people, Lawrence had been after his dad's recipe from the time the son was a pup. In fact, at age fifteen, Lawrence had been bribed by a rival trapper to steal the recipe, in exchange for drugs. Only later did Lawrence really want the recipe just for trapping. But the gnarled old woodsman never forgave the boy; and he was vindictive in his revenge. Not only wouldn't Kurt reveal the recipe, but he didn't refuse outright. He just kept delaying – kept saying, "Soon Son, someday soon." Year after year for four decades. Just as some parents taunt and control their kids with promises of bequeathing money, so too Kurt worked his bile on Lawrence. Then, suddenly Kurt was dead. And the secret of his bait died with him. I was present at the wake and had a chance to look over Kurt's workbench. It contained mason jars of meat from various animals, all in a couple of inches of water, sitting in sunlight, so putrid they were just masses of goo. Also on his bench were bottles of beaver castor and scent glands from mountain goat, moose, mink and weasel, as well as numerous other things that weren't labeled and which I couldn't identify. Just how he mixed all of these together to achieve a final blend, I had no idea. I guess Lawrence didn't either. I've heard it said he tried to poison himself afterward, out of disappointment. But my own guess is that poisoning himself was just an accidental result of fooling around with Kurt's ingredients. That putrid meat alone was enough to cause gangrene in half the population of Montana.

In addition to covey sets, I also occasionally used trail sets. After finding a new trail, I'd walk along it, checking the ground for bear tracks, and trail-side trees for bear hair. Now and then, I'd find a rough-barked conifer on which a bear had rubbed itself, leaving behind small tufts of hair and bite marks. Both grizzly and black bears could be any color. But only grizzly hair had light tips. Their tracks also differed in size and shape, with grizzlies tending to be larger, with proportionately longer claws on their hands.

Once I found a well-traveled trail, I searched for what I called chutes – narrow places on the trail that prevented a bear from walking around any obstruction in the trail. If there weren't steep banks or trees to keep a bear on the trail, I felled small trees on each side of the trail, piling them high to funnel the bear where I wanted it. Again, I often made use of a bear's preference for stepping over small logs, rather than on them. In the middle of the chute, two branches laid were across the trail, eighteen inches apart. In that space, the snare was hidden – the opposite end of the cable having been cinched to a standing tree or to a log *drag*.

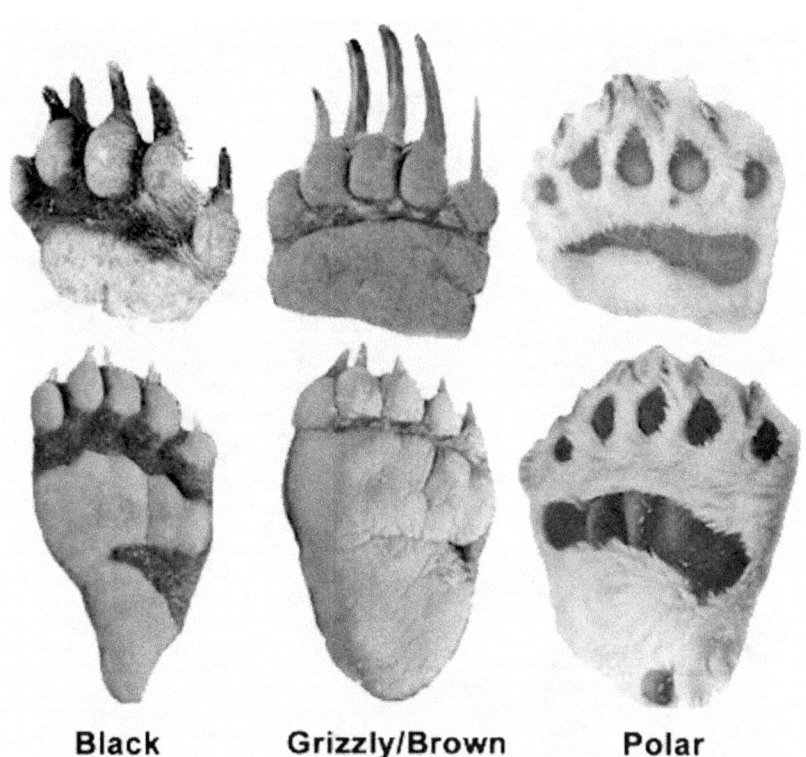

Black   **Grizzly/Brown**   **Polar**

4.7a: Bear hands (top row) and feet (bottom row). The finger-claws of a black or polar bear are about as long as its finger pads; a grizzly's finger claws are up to 3 times as long as its finger pads. In all three species, toe claws tend to be shorter than toe pads (Stringham 2010).

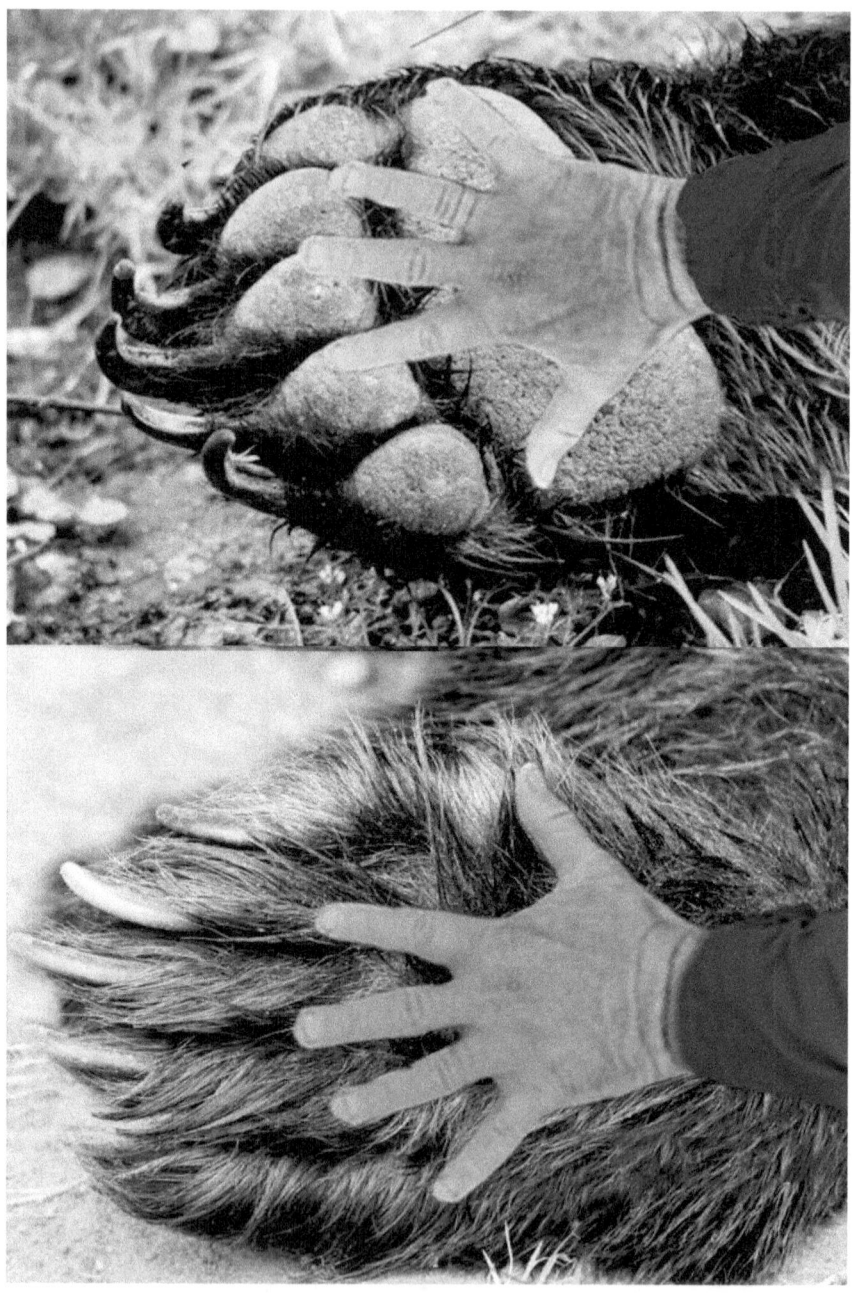

4.7b: Grizzly hand vs. human hand (iStock images. Heidloss Tilo & Felix Geringswald photos).

4.7c: Footprints are easiest to follow when made in firm sand.

4.8a: While I watched from over 100 yards away, a grizzly bear scent-marked this birch tree, leaving bite marks and hair on the trunk. During spring when bears are shedding, hair comes off in gobs.

4.8b: Rest of the year few hairs are left each time, although they
accumulate over time as multiple bears rub on the same spots.

A variant on the trail set was a bridge set. Bears like bridges. Even
a bear that readily plunges into a river after salmon is often reluctant
to wade across the same stream merely to reach the other side, especially if there's a fallen log on which to walk across. A pit can be
chopped into the center of such a log, and a trap placed there,
provided that there are obstructions along the log to force the bear to
step right on top of the trap. Or the snare can be placed at one end of
the log, in a spot likely to receive a bear's foot.

Trail sets like that don't need to be baited to work. But, occasionally I used baits to help assure that the animal stepped right were I
wanted it too. This was done by hanging bait from a tree limb so that
a bear would rise up on its hind feet and try to reach the bait with its
hands. Walking around like that, looking up, bears don't necessarily
pay much attention to where they put their feet.

4.8c: Grizzly sniffing mark tree.

4.9: Snare lying on the ground between two sticks, as it is being covered with leaves as camouflage. The free end will be attached by another cable to a tree (illustration).

* * *

Catching a bear in a snare is a bit like catching one by the tail. That's when the fun really begins. One of our most exciting captures occurred when I teamed up with another greenhorn trapper whom I'll call George. The black bear we caught was both ferocious and frightened, perhaps terrified, as we approached. At first, it jumped behind the tree to which it was staked, lying low to hide as well as possible. Then, when we got too close, it jumped up and tried to flee. Failing that, it charged, as if to attack. Time and again it lunged, each time jerking its snared right foreleg back under its belly toward its tail so hard that the animal did a nose dive or a front flip, landing on its back. Its wrist, probably already raw when we arrived, was soon bloody.

While George hid behind a tree, waiting for me to get into position, I circled around on one side, keeping the bear's attention on me, as it lunged again and again. No matter how much my intellect told me that the cable was too strong to break and that I was perfectly safe, every ferocious lunge by the bear was absolutely terrifying, at least for a second or two. I can't say that I ever got used to that. I just took it in stride, like all the hundreds of other biologists who have live-trapped bears. Brave? No more so than drivers on highways who approach one another in opposite directions at a combined speed of over one hundred miles per hour, yet separated by just a few feet. If a tire blows out or a freak accident occurs, drivers and passengers could be crippled or killed. Yet few drivers worry about such unlikely events. Likewise, trappers who use well-designed equipment, in good condition, don't worry about cables snapping. Not very often, anyway. The shock absorbers I mentioned not only minimize injury to a bear. They also protect the cable from excessive strain.

In any event, as I circled this bear and drew its attention away from George, he stepped out into the open, raised the capture gun, sighting in on the bear's rump, and blasted it. Shortly thereafter, it passed out.

Houdini

After capturing and handling numerous black bears, I thought I'd mastered the art of trapping well enough to handle even a grizzly bear. So far, we'd never found one in any of our traps. But we were always aware of that possibility, and very cautious every time we approached a trapped bear, fearing that if it charged, its foot might pull free from the snare or the snare might break free from its anchor, despite all our preparations to make sure this couldn't happen. Only once did our preparations fail; but the incident plagued me with nightmares for months afterward.

As expected of a trapped bear, the first griz I ever snared went berserk with fear, frustration and anger, tearing up or breaking all the vegetation within reach. Even trees 4" to 6" in diameter were snapped off several feet above the ground! As we approached this bear, it leaped up and charged – only to be jerked off its feet as it reached the end of the cable-slack and the trapped paw was jerked back under the bear, flipping it onto its back. After two more fruitless lunges, the bruin reversed directions and raced away from us. Expecting to see the bear again flipped head over heels, we were horrified to see the anchor tree ripped up by its roots and dragged away.

We normally anchored each snare to a tree over 6" in diameter. In this case, however, the only available anchor was an alder. While none of its multiple trunks were more than two inches in diameter, its stem appeared large enough and well-enough rooted to serve our needs. Oops! Had the roots given way when the bear charged toward us, rather than away, we would have quickly been converted from flesh and bone biologists to bear dung and newspaper statistics.

As soon as the alder tangled in other brush, briefly anchoring the bear again, we shot the bruin with a tranquilizer dart and kept our distance until it passed out.

Free-roaming bears

By now, you can understand why we preferred darting bears only after they were securely snared. However, biologists are sometimes forced to tranquilize a bear that they can't trap beforehand. That's how Will Troyer handled bears at Katmai National Park – sneaking up and firing a dart into a muscled rump or shoulder, then waiting for it to fall asleep, praying that it wouldn't get angry and retaliate before succumbing to the drug.

You've probably heard so-called Polish jokes, like *"How do Polacks screw in a light bulb? One stands on a ladder and holds the bulb in the socket while four others turn the ladder."* So you might appreciate how a web photo, allegedly of a Polish biologist, inspired our own joke: *"How does a Polack capture a bear? Shoot it with a tranquilizer dart, then run like 'ell and keep out of reach until the bear falls over asleep."*

We darted bears using a modified rifle or shotgun. Our gun's firing pin hit a 22-caliber blank charge which fired a dart up to twenty feet through the air. Each dart was roughly four inches long and no more than half-an-inch in diameter. The central cylinder held the drug. A thick needle tip was screwed onto the front of the cylinder, and a tail onto the rear. The tail contained another 22-blank which exploded on impact, driving a plunger forward, through the tube, forcing the drug out of the syringe and into the bear. The tail ended in a tuft of red yarn which steadied the dart's flight, much like feathers on the end of an arrow.

Cabin Eater

The only griz we snared on purpose was a huge male known as Cabin Eater. On the north side of our study area, near the Canadian border, was a beautiful little valley where horses grazed in creek-bottom meadows where the grass was waist-high. For some reason, the weather there was much cooler and more pleasant than in the valleys where we normally worked. Along the creek – possibly Geiffer Creek – was a series of small cabins, most inhabited only during summer. Winter snows were so deep that few people braved them. Yet, never have I so wished to settle down and live anywhere. Rarely have I ever felt more at home.

Apparently, this grizzly did too. He'd break into a cabin through one window, fool around inside, exit through a second window, re-enter through a third, and so on until most of the windows had been torn out. Some of these windows were so small that he must have had a devil of a time squeezing through, but somehow he managed, even if he had to tear the window frame out in the process. I suspect that it was a kind of game for him, smashing through glass and passing through new holes like that. Somehow, he was never cut by the glass; at least we never found a drop of blood. Not at the windows, and not in the kitchens where he tore everything apart and ate nearly any food. I found one peanut butter jar which he'd broken open. The jar was completely clean, with hardly a trace of peanut butter. How he had managed to lick the glass without cutting himself is still a mystery.

After demolishing several cabins, the Cabin Eater was finally trapped in a snare. We found him the following morning and approached cautiously. He went crazy, roar-moaning, thrashing everything within reach. It took all our courage to continue walking through the brush toward this fury incarnate, never sure that he wouldn't break free and kill us all. Every gun we possessed was loaded, cocked, aimed and ready to fire.

If we'd been frightened by the sounds Cabin Eater made, we were a hundred-fold more frightened by the sight of this raging, behemoth. Every tree within his reach had already been massacred. All trunks less than about four inches in diameter had been snapped off, much as a person might snap stems of grass. Somewhat larger trunks had been shredded by bites and roundhouse swats, leaving splinters up to an inch thick, two inches wide sticking out in all directions.

Yet, Cabin Eater succumbed to the drugs as readily as any black bear and remained sedated as we used a big canvas sling and come-along to slide him up a ramp into the back of a pickup.

Not sure how long the grizzly would remain quiet, we raced over washboard roads and dodged potholes, on our way back to the valley of North Fork of the Flathead River, where there were few people who could be bothered by the grizzly.

Once, during the trip, Cabin Eater stirred, as though waking up. I nearly panicked and almost jumped out of the pickup while it was still racing down the gravel road. However, quickly recognizing that the griz wasn't really awake yet, I gave him a second dose of sedative. Thereafter, he remained quiet even as we slid him back out of the pickup onto the ground. By then, it was Miller Time, and the other fellows left. I remained behind to protect Cabin Eater in case another bear or even a pack of wolves or puma came along that could attack while he was helpless.

Apparently, the second dose of the drug hit Cabin Eater much stronger than the first. Nearly two hours passed before he could sit up, then stumble around on wobbly legs. Not knowing whether I had more than seconds to get beyond his reach, I gunned my engine and roared down the road – only to slow, then stop three hundred yards away. Cabin Eater was on his feet, now moving with smooth coordination. Instead of chasing me, he just stood and watched for a few minutes, then began feeding on the lush growth of huckleberries that lined the margins of the narrow dirt road. Slowly, Cabin Eater worked his way closer and closer to me. Slowly, I inched farther way, keeping enough distance between us to provide ample time for a getaway, should he charge. Fortunately, he never did. The last I saw of Cabin Eater was when he melted into the forest, like butter melting into hot a hot biscuit.

Sweet Dreams Boobaloo

The first immobilizing drug I used on the bears – while working with Kelly – was succinylcholine chloride, brand name sucostrin, an artificial form of curare. Curare is a plant poison used by Natives in South America to kill prey. It paralyzes voluntary (striated) muscle, which includes all the limb and torso muscles. So long as the dose is light, it doesn't impair respiration, and the animal remains fully conscious, aware of how it is being handled, feeling pain and subject to stress. However, if the dose is too strong, paralyzing the diaphragm, the animal can suffocate unless given artificial respiration.

Each bear was carefully monitored, but sometimes the dose was too high and the bear had trouble breathing. This happened on one of my last days helping Kelly back in California in 1969. Desperate to save it, we opened the trap's door, pulled the bear out of the trap, and lowered it to the ground. Immediately, Kelly laid his jacket under the bear's head to protect its eyes from vegetation and soil. I dropped to the ground by the bear's chest, lay on my back, placed my feet on its chest, and began pumping with my legs, providing artificial respiration. Half-an-hour passed before the tranquilizer wore off and the bear woke up. By that time, I was too tired to even stand up and run for the pickup. The bear came up suddenly and I was afraid it would maul me. But the experience of having been helpless in our hands for an hour may have convinced the bear that we were too powerful to mess with. It staggered over me and off into the forest.

The bear wasn't the only casualty of that incident. In my haste to save its life, I didn't notice that it was lying in a patch of poison oak brush. Within a few days, nearly every inch of my face, neck and torso were covered with suppurating blisters whose itching threatened to drive me mad until I was finally able to get a prescription for cortisone. Even with an injection and ointment, the next two weeks were pure misery. I couldn't help but wonder whether the bear knew it had been revenged.

* * *

To avoid any more respiratory problems wildlife biologists switched to sernyln which didn't just immobilize bears; it also tranquilized them and probably made them a bit high, judging from their behavior and the fact that that's how people react. But that had its own problems.

All wildlife tranquilizers have to be treated with respect, due both to dangers from the drugs and too unpredictable responses by the animals. M-99 and other morphine derivatives, for instance, are extremely toxic to people. Even a single drop can be fatal to a person, as some people, including experienced veterinarians, have found out the hard way. An ideal drug would be harmless to people and to wildlife, causing only deep sleep or paralysis of skeletal muscles, but not the diaphragm, without any side effects. Short of that ideal, we prefer drugs that are harmless to people in the small doses one gets by scratching yourself against a needle, as sometimes happens in the rush of handling an animal. Likewise, we prefer drugs with a wide safety margin, so that if we underestimate the animal's weight, too little drug just slows it down, and too much merely keeps it quiet longer, without danger of dying.

Data Collection

Trapping and handling bears, moose and other large wildlife is usually done by a team. There's a lot to do, and sometimes a lot of gear to carry. Worse, such large animals are heavy and hard to roll over or lift. While one is tranquilized, biologists take numerous body measurements, and samples of hair and other tissues for DNA finger-printing and for analyzing the animal's health and nutritional status. Among the things measured are some of the same blood variables which are assessed for human health. Fluid and tissue samples can also reveal other aspects of physiological status (e.g., pregnant or in estrus).

As soon as a bear collapsed, we put a clean cloth under and over its head to protect its eyes and face. If the immobilizing drug prevented the bear from blinking, one of us periodically kept them moist with drops of sterile saline or Murine. We wanted to be thorough and gather as much useful information as possible. But just as with a human patient under sedation, we wanted to finish up as quickly as possible to minimize physical and emotional trauma. Some tranquilizers put a bear to sleep; but others like curare just temporarily paralyzed the animal, while leaving it conscious of everything happening to it as we conducted measurements, extracted a tiny premolar tooth, and tattooed its lip.

Tattoo pliers have wide needle-studded jaws. Quarter-inch long needles on the lower jaw form a unique ID number. We smeared the pins with ink, pulled the animal's upper lip between the pliers, then squeezed them shut. If you've ever had a dentist jab a needle into your mouth to inject novocaine, I doubt you enjoyed the experience. That was probably a very thin needle, handled by a professional who was trying very hard to be gentle, based on hundreds of times practicing on other people – each of whom could scream bloody murder and hire a lawyer if it hurt too much.

Now imagine not one thin needle, but a couple of dozen thick needles, handled by an amateur. Imagine these needles jammed not into your gums, which are relatively insensitive but jabbed into your ultrasensitive lips with all the finesse of a ditch-digger using a pickaxe. If someone even hinted about doing that to me, I'd start imagining ways to peel off their skin inch by inch. The thought that bears might have similar fantasies about me didn't help me sleep at night.

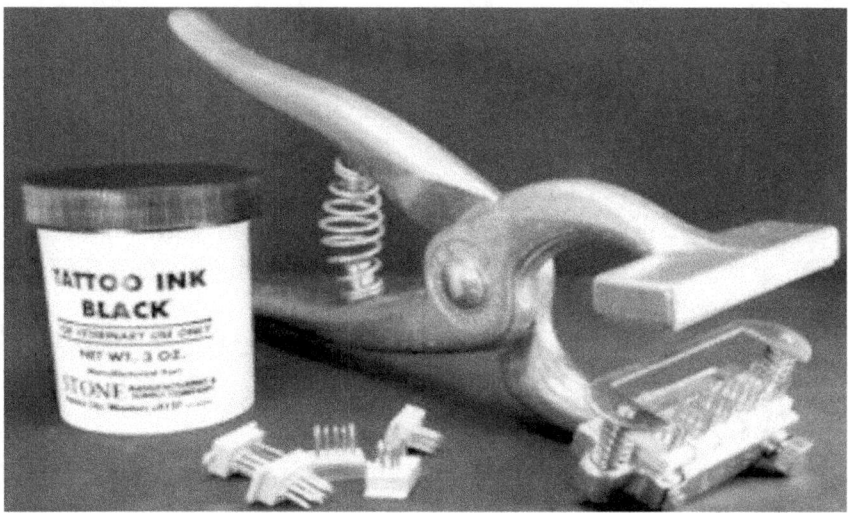

4.10: Tattoo pliers: The needles can be seen on the lower part of the devise (Credit: www.wildlifecontrolsupplies.com; www.stonemfg.net/brochures.html Stone manufacturing Co.).

Bear Back Riding

One of the best compromise drugs was sernylan. Unfortunately, it was virtually identical to the street drug known as Angel Dust and classified as a narcotic. That forced us to handle the tranquilizers with very tight security, documenting that we never misused them and protected them against theft. Sernylan was widely used with great success on bears until someone noted that people high on Angel Dust became violently aggressive, then speculated that the same thing might be true for bears. They jumped to the conclusion that some of the bears which had attacked people had previously been drugged with sernylan by biologists. However, so far as I know, no bear tranquilized with sernylan ever attacked anyone, or at least not within the year or two following tranquilization. But rumors acquire a life of their own, and the harder one tries to refute them, the more people assume you're trying to do a cover-up; so they believe the fake news. The result was a virtual banning of sernylan for use on bears.

One of the first alternatives in common use was a blend of ketamine hydrochloride and rompun. My initial experience using this drug mix was while I was assisting Chuck Jonkel. We were on the North Fork of the Flathead River, just west of Glacier National Park in Montana, and just south of the Canadian Border.

After the tranquilized black bear had been still for at least fifteen minutes, Chuck inserted a crocodile-head-shaped metal tag into each of the bear's ears, squeezing the tag's jaws closed with pliers. The teeth of the tag bit into the skin and cartilage of the ear, and the bear began struggling weakly.

"Chuck, this animal's waking up!" I warned. Chuck returned the tagging pliers back to the huge tackle box used for carrying our equipment and supplies.

"Well, don't come unglued," he chided in his usual unflappable way, picking up a pair of tattoo pliers. "It's just involuntary muscle movements."

By now the bear's legs were moving like those of a dog dreaming – perhaps of running through the forest. Chuck inserted a pair of tattoo needles that would mark this bear as number NF45 (NF = North Fork). Then he rubbed each needle tip with thick green ink. The bear's head was now moving too much for Chuck to tattoo its lip, so he demanded that I hold the head still.

I straddled the bear, slipping my arms under its armpits and hammer-locking my hands behind its head. Chuck lifted the upper lip with his left hand while positioning the pliers with his right. But the bear pulled loose. "Hold it still!" Chuck commanded.

"I'm trying. But it's waking up."

"Don't exaggerate. It's still a long ways from recovered. Just hold it still so I can tattoo the lip."

With that, Chuck lifted the lip again, inserted it between the two jaws and clamped down.

The bear jerked onto its feet, with me on its back, still holding it in a hammerlock, which forced its head down near the ground.

"Can't you hold it still?" Chuck complained gruffly.

"This animal is awake!"

By this time, Chuck was really exasperated by my bearanoia. Under sernylan, movements like this occurred while a bear was still in the grip of the tranquilizer and portended no danger.

"Just let the animal go. It'll fall over," Chuck instructed me.

Had we been using sernylan, I might have complied. But this was a new combination of drugs, and we didn't really know the pattern of recovery.

"Not until you have your gun ready," I resisted, anxious for whatever security the 44-magnum represented.

"Oh, for gosh sakes! Who do you think I am, Dirty Harry?" Shaking his head in frustration, Chuck pulled out the pistol and pointed it at the bear, sure that I was one of the most timid grad students he'd ever suffered through.

"Cock it," I demanded. More head shaking, but Chuck complied, backing up until he was about five feet from the bear.

"Okay, on the count of three. One ... two ... three!" I let go and jumped back in the same instant.

"See, I told you ..." Chuck started to say, certain that the bear would have fallen back down on the ground. But it was gone. Disappeared, like a puff of smoke – whereupon we dubbed him Smokey Bear. We heard a crash of brush and looked up to see the bear emerge on the far side of a ravine, maybe thirty feet away, running full bore.

Chuck's face paled for just a moment, as he uncocked the pistol and shoved it back into his holster.

Tension drained out of both of us and transformed into laughter. Nervous, *glad, very glad to be alive*, laughter. "I guess it was awake," Chuck admitted, perhaps thinking of how he'd had his hands in the bear's month just seconds earlier. How easily it could have crunched both of them and mauled both of us, had it been so inclined.

Fortunately, there are now much better drugs available – such as telazol or carfentanil – which are safer for both people and wildlife.

Injuries and Fatalities

In later years, additional precautions were taken to further minimize stress on the animals we captured. For example, snares have been padded. Nevertheless, recent research has revealed a variety of traumas that we overlooked or underestimated. In 2008, Marc Cattet, a University of Saskatchewan biologist and veterinarian, reported that bears that have violently fought to escape a snare suffer muscle damage. For up to five weeks after capture, a bear can remain stiff and sore. This reduces how much it travels by up to 50%, and probably the efficiency with which it forages and meets other needs for itself and any cubs. Traumatized bears lost body weight and may have lost cubs. Whereas we always assumed that any such traumas were over in a few weeks at most, new evidence shows that impairments can last for years and that they accumulate if the bear is captured repeatedly. Trapping bears in culverts or barrels, or darting bears from a helicopter, also produce persistent stress. So the search for better methods continues.

My colleague Lynn Rogers prefers to tame bears so much that they tolerate his touch. While a bear is licking up sunflower seeds from his hand, he slips a radio collar over its neck with his other hand. Unfortunately, the technique hasn't caught on, in part because of an erroneous belief among troglodytic wildlife biologists that taming bears makes them more dangerous. In fact, the reverse is often true, as many of the incidents in this book demonstrate.

4.11: Sue Mansfield holds radio collar in preparation for mounting it on a bear that has not been captured or tranquilized.

4.12: Assisted by Sue Mansfield, Lynn Rogers slips a radio collar around the neck of this black bear.

4.13: Lynn Rogers attaches the radio collar.

Two other tactics for minimizing trauma while gathering data are camera traps and hair traps. A typical camera trap is a trail cam that takes a photo or video clip each time its motion sensor is triggered. The resulting photo can reveal which bear passed, as well as the date and time of passage, and perhaps whether it had companions. A series of such images might also reveal that a bear is followed by a fellow bear or by a wolf pack, or vice versa. Granted, a lot of bears look similar, making it difficult for us to distinguish among individuals based solely on trail cam photos. However, that problem can be minimized if the cam is aimed at a hair trap. DNA fingerprinting of hair samples can reliably distinguish individual bears, and thus help us also distinguish them in photos. Hair is usually trapped by stretching barbed wire between trees surrounding a bait so that any bear trying to get the bait pushes up against the barbs, which snag small clumps of hair. Alternately, barbed wire or sticky duct tape can be wrapped around a tree trunk where bears spontaneously rub. Here too, hair is caught on the barbs or on the tape.

Especially during the 1960s and 1970s while techniques and drug dosages were being worked out, a few bears did die from an overdose. That risk declined over time as we learned better to judge each bear's body weight – which is the primary determinant of drug dosage – and how to adjust dosages according to physiological conditions such as exhaustion, body fat index, and pregnancy or lactation. As new immobilizing or tranquilizing drugs were invented, we also tested those to find which ones were safest for animals and people. As mentioned earlier, even a tiny drop of some drugs such as M99 could be fatal to a person. Fortunately, there is no evidence that being trapped and handled in any of these ways has ever made a bear more aggressive.

So far as I know, no biologist has ever been seriously injured while trapping and marking bears; and I know of only one case of a bystander being attacked. Whenever a bear trap is set, signs are put up warning people to stay away, lest they be mauled or provoke the bear into injuring itself. The signs are usually left up for a day or two after the bear has recovered, in case it doesn't quickly leave the area, lest someone stumbles on a bruin that is dazed or cranky. Unfortunately, though, one man was killed when he approached a recently released grizzly, despite having been warned to stay away.

By chance, his widow learned that I serve as an Expert Witness in court cases involving bears. She phoned and asked me to help her win a settlement from the U.S. Fish & Wildlife Service whose biologists had captured and marked the bear. However, during several phone calls, I heard no grief for her lost husband, only what sounded like greed. Furthermore, as best I could learn, her husband's fate was largely his own fault. Apparently, a jury agreed.

Where Angels Fear to Tread

The border between Montana and Idaho follows a mountain spine zig-zagging south to north until it hits Canada. Branching off the spine is a series of rib-like ridges. Western ribs slope down into Idaho; eastern ridges slope down into Montana. One of my jobs for Chuck was hiking the northern Montana ribs searching for bears, especially grizzlies. On a typical hike, I'd park at the eastern tip of a rib and follow its southern slope upwards and westwards to the spine. The next day, I'd cross to the northern slope of that same rib and hike back eastwards to its tip, where I'd left my vehicle. While hiking one side of a rib, I couldn't see much on that slope; but I could get good views across the adjacent valley to its opposite slope. By moving from rib to rib, I was able to search each valley with reasonable thoroughness.

On one hike, it was late afternoon before I got close to the spine, maybe 500' vertically below the 7000' peak of Mt. Waab. It rose about 3 miles WNW of Mt. Thompson-Seton. Waab was a bear cub about which naturalist Ernest Thompson-Seton had written at the start of the 20th Century. His books on North American wildlife were some of the best references available in the English language even in the mid-20th century.

Mornings and evenings were often the best time to see bears, so I stopped hiking around 4 pm and quickly set up camp. One evening, my supper was a chunk of corn bread, along with thick slabs of cheddar cheese and Hormel canned ham. With those in hand, I walked a few hundred yards to the crest of a cliff. That spot proved a superb view of the valley below, which stretched out miles to the east. The forest was broken up by avalanche chutes and meadows with low enough vegetation that I could see a few black bears through my binoculars and spotting scope.

I became so engrossed watching them and taking notes that I didn't notice the passage of time until the sun set. The valley below me filled with shadow, like molasses' filling a bowl. Gathering my gear, I turned around and started toward camp … only to discover that the slope was hidden in such a dark shadow that my camp was invisible. I kept searching until the night was as black as the inside of a cave. Without stars to see for orientation, I couldn't tell which way was which. Wandering around hoping to stumble into camp, I'd be just as likely to stumble over the cliff where I'd sat watching bears.

This reminded me of a similar situation when my father got stuck out overnight in Colorado's Estes Park in 1948. He and another fire-fighter had hiked into the mountains to extinguish a small lightening-strike fire. By the time they'd used up all their water, one small spot was still smoking. It was about 30' up an aspen tree, in the crotch where the trunk forked into two thick branches. To extinguish that last spark, Dad climbed up and peed on it. He and his partner were still miles from a road when dark hit. The two men stumbled around for awhile before Dad decided that continuing would be too danger-ous. His partner didn't want to stop, but Dad prevailed. When dawn came, they found they were about 6' from the lip of a high cliff. A few more steps the previous night and they'd have gone over.

Rather than risk a similar fate or even lesser injury, I finally sat down and waited for the moon to rise. When it finally did, there still wasn't enough light to find camp. But I could see the shine of snow on the mountain peak. By that time, the salty ham had made me so thirsty that I could hardly think of anything else except water. Using sticks like a blind man's canes, I worked my way up the slope, some of it quite steep, until I reached snow. I gorged on it, sucking it or chewing and swallowing it for water until my tongue was numb and my brain felt like an icicle had been driven into it. By that time my hands were also numb and my body shivering.

Yet nearly an hour passed before my thirst diminished enough that I cared about the cold. Carefully moving lower on the slope, I found a dry spot in the lee of several boulders which provided scant protection from the wind. Gathering whatever dry brush I could find, I pulled it into the sheltered spot, preparing to make a fire. More than half-an-hour passed with my fingers tucked into my arm pits before they were flexible enough to hold a match. I no sooner got a fire started though than a gust of wind blew it out. I was nearly out of matches before a flame finally continued burning for at least fifteen minutes before waning and finally disappearing. Fortunately though, the damp wood continued to smolder for the rest of the night.

No matter where I positioned myself around the smudge, the smoke followed me. The only way I could keep from having to breathe smoke constantly was to lie with my mouth practically on the ground.

4.14: Lightening storm I endured on Mount Thompson Seton (artistic recreation).

It would be ironic and perhaps fatal if a grizzly showed up here after all the days I'd spent looking for them without finding even one. What my eyes couldn't find, the remains of my ham might lure. Once a bear sniffed out that meat and consumed it, following my scent would lead it directly to me. I kept praying that the smoke would keep bears away. But if one did show up in the night and approached me, I would have to hope that the smudge had been producing enough heat to keep my fingers thawed, so that I could shoot the .357 magnum pistol I carried for protection.

Unable to sleep while listening intently for bears, taking fright every time I heard any stray sound, I lay shivering, shaking and choking on smoke until dawn. As the eastern horizon split into a voluptuous smile, and a warm tongue of golden light licked the valley awake, I was amazed to see that I was little more than 150' feet directly above my camp. Within ten minutes, I was back there, crawling into my sleeping bag, falling asleep for several hours, without stopping even long enough to move the remains of my ham a safe distance from camp.

I awoke to find the mountain top completely shrouded in fog so thick that it cut visibility to no more than 200'. I wasn't particularly worried since I had a snug camp, with plenty of food and water. After the previous night's ordeal, I was just as happy to rest there all day, expecting sunshine the next morning. Fat chance. I awoke to an even thicker fog. By the third day, I was out of food and anxious to get back to the trapping cabin lest someone think I had gotten lost or injured. Having a search party called out on my behalf would have been a trifle embarrassing. I packed up, checked my map and compass bearings, then continued on my planned route to the northern side of the rib I'd been following, whereupon I intended to hike back eastwards to the road and my vehicle.

Unbeknownst to me, the rock around there was heavy in iron, which threw my compass way off. While I thought I was hiking east along the north side of the original rib-ridge, I actually hiked west across the mountain spine separating Montana from Idaho. When the fog briefly parted enough to reveal a gravel road in the valley below me, I thought it was the tributary of the North Fork road where I had started a few days earlier. I fought my way a few thousand feet downwards through thick vegetation, to the road. For the next hour, I searched along it, trying in vain to find where I'd left the bicycle which I had ridden from the trapping cabin. At first, I thought someone had stolen the bike. But I soon realized that the valley didn't look quite as I remembered it; and the gravel covering the road was much larger than I recalled – too large to be easily ridden over on a bike. Finally, a pickup appeared in the distance, kicking up a huge cloud of dust as it approached. I flagged down the elderly driver and asked how far I was from the cabin. She laughed and said I was on the wrong side of the Continental Divide, in Idaho.

That left me with two choices. Hitch a ride to the nearest town and call Chuck to arrange a ride back to the North Fork – which might brand me as a fool and get me evicted from the team. Or retrace my route, hopefully without getting lost any worse than I already was. It had been raining all day through the fog. So the chest-high bear grass and other vegetation through which I had climbed on my way down to the road was still bent over, showing signs of my passage. Backtracking, racing uphill as fast as I could climb, I made it to the top of the spine just before dark.

My body was trembling with fatigue. My legs felt like jelly and my mind was woozy. I may have already been on the verge of hypothermia, and I'd certainly end up there if I didn't get shelter. Finally finding a spot of bare rock where I could pitch a tent, I wasted no time in erecting it and crawling in. Stripping off my sodden clothing, I wiggled into the bag, thanking God that I'd had sense enough to carry it in a waterproof stuff sack.

However, I wasn't thanking God for long. Within an hour, the constant rain created a small stream running through my campsite. Had the foot of the tent not been zipped shut, my air mattress would have floated me right on out of the tent, much as happened at age 14 when I was a Boy Scout camping in the Sierras. That's when I learned the value of digging a shallow ditch around my tent. But on this night in Montana, camping on bedrock, digging a ditch hadn't been an option.

Then, as though Satan had decided to enjoy a little more fun at my expense, every muscle from my waist to my toes locked up in a charley horse. Normally, I could stop cramps by fighting my way onto my feet and stretching out the muscles. But in the middle of the cloud burst, this wasn't possible without guaranteeing hypothermia. Writhing and groaning, sometimes nearly screaming in agony, I had no choice but to suffer the torments of hell. At some point, I recalled that cramps were often caused to dehydration. My skin being soaked with rain all day hadn't necessarily kept my inner tissues moist enough. I leaned over my mattress and sucked water into my mouth, along with dirt and pine needles. Yet, another eternity passed before the cramps finally subsided.

I was one very wet, very bedraggled cowboy before I made it back to the trapping cabin. Fortunately, the potbellied stove was glowing red with heat, and I soaked it up like a loaf of baking bread.

Taking pity on me, Chuck gave me an easier assignment for my last week on the job. Instead of camping out, I'd have shelter in the fire lookout station atop 7,815 ft Mount Thompson Seton. Although no longer used as a fire lookout, the building was still weather-proof. Each of the four walls consisted mainly of large windows, providing a superb view in all directions. My assignment was to look out each of those windows every hour, searching for bears.

I don't recall seeing many bears or other wildlife. But I did get my fill of watching lightening. One of the first things I noticed upon reaching the building was the presence of several half-inch thick copper lightening rods running from the roof down into bedrock. At the time, I suspected that was overkill. But I learned better when a thunderstorm hit and lightning bolts started flashing through the clouds. If a lightning bolt struck through the building, I didn't want to be standing on the floor, lest that ground me to the underlying bedrock. All the furniture was metal. Sitting or standing on that would be just as bad. Somehow, I had to suspend myself a few feet above the floor. The building had exposed overhead joists running from one wall to the next. Using a rope, I hoisted the metal bed into the air, then climbed aboard to enjoy the fireworks. By sheer chance, I happened to have a pocket cassette tape player with me. Beethoven's Fifth Symphony, the 1812 Overture by Tchaikovsky, and a Concerto by Bruckner were the perfect accompaniment to the storm. The building was surrounded by a boiling mixture of clouds whose colors ranged from pure white to gold to blue to nearly black. The lightening quickly advanced from single bolts to a golden network that flashed almost without ceasing. Thunder shook the cabin like an angry bear. It was terrifying. It was glorious. It was the finest send-off imaginable if this were my last hour on earth.

Multimedia for Chapter 4.

5

EYEBALL TO EYEBALL

WITH BEARS IN THEIR DENS

5.1: Lynn Rogers using a yagi antenna to detect the radio signal from a bear's collar. The beep-beep-beep signal captured by the antenna flows through a cable to the receiver which he's holding to his ear (NABC).

A fter my stint on Mt. Thompson-Seton was done, I spent the rest of the summer of 1976 assisting Chuck's crew in capturing bears. Then, after a hiatus of two years with little field work, I began working toward my doctoral degree at the University of Tennessee. Although my own research was with grizzly bears in Montana and Wyoming during summers, I occasionally assisted other grad students in capturing and marking black bears in Great Smoky Mountains National Park (1978-1983) and later in New York's Adirondack Park (1985-86).

Once a bear was immobilized, tattooed, examined, sampled (blood and other tissues), measured and ear-tagged, we fitted it with a collar containing a radio transmitter. The transmissions were monitored with a yagi antenna – like a TV antenna with shortened elements (= horizontal cross bars) and less spacing between elements. We drove forest logging roads or hiked through the wilds, or flew in a small plane such as a Supercub or Cessna 180, searching for a radio signal, noting the direction from which it emanated. After detecting the signal from enough directions to triangulate the bear's position, we were often able to hike in and spot the animal, then document its location and the type of habitat it was using. Then off to do the same thing for several more animals.

Through the 1960s and early 1970s, collar batteries lasted only a few months, which created the problem of having to trap the bear again in order to remove its collar or replace it with one having fresh batteries. That problem waned when more durable batteries became available. By the 1980s, most "recaptures" were done without actually recapturing the bear. Instead, we waited until winter and followed its radio signal to the bear's den.

Hibernating bears were hardest to reach when they denned in a tree – usually one with a diameter of at least four feet, and a hollow core. Rotting of a tree's core often began when a big branch broke off, leaving a stub that was easily penetrated by molds, bacteria, and fungi which fed on the wood, weakening and softening it enough that the rotting wood could be dug out by birds or mammals that sought shelter within the trunk. Over decades, the entire core might rot, sometimes down more than 50 feet. A bear dug down into it and prepared its winter bed.

5.2: Black bear in den (NABC).

5.3: Black bear in tree den (courtesy NPS.gov, Glacier National Park).

5.4a: Biologist Lisa Bates investigating a tree den in Maine, in partnership with Professor George Matula, Unity College. We did the same thing in Tennessee [Courtesy Grandfather Restoration Project].

5.4b: Black bear in tree den (Frank T. van Manen photo).

Such den trees were common in Great Smokey Mountains National Park. To reach a tree den, we shot an arrow up over a limb of the tree which was higher than the entrance hole were the old branch had been. Attached to the arrow was a strong string, which was attached to an eighth-inch nylon cord, which was attached to half-inch climbing rope. Once the arrow returned to earth, we used the string to pull the cord, which pulled the rope. Tying the two ends together at ground level produced a complete loop of rope around the limb and back to ground level. One of us climbed the rope using climbing gear until we reached the opening in the trunk. Then the daring biologist had to use another rope to lower oneself down into the den until one reached the bear. It was tranquilized and processed in place. Small wonder we preferred bears which denned in the ground.

Fortunately, we didn't always have to disturb bears to get the information needed. If our main objective was to determine whether a bear was alive and had cubs, we could learn that by inserting a microphone into the den. When cubs vocalized it was sometimes possible to distinguish among their voices and thus get a minimum count of the number of cubs. That information could then be linked with data on food supply to test a theory that well-nourished females gave birth to more cubs, or that their cubs survived better.

In my limited experience, denned black bears tend to be highly alert at temperatures at or above -10° F. On a number of occasions, a bear detected the sound of my feet crunching snow even while I was at least two hundred yards away. A few of them burst out of the den and fled, huffing and clacking jaws in fear. Once in the Smokey Mountains, our approach spooked two yearling cubs, which were apparently more alert than their mother. While she stayed in her den, the cubs raced away up a mountainside. Fearing that they would end up stranded away from their den and die of exposure, one of the other grad students and I followed them, expecting that they would eventually tire so much we would be able to just pick them up and haul them back to the den. (Yes, we really were that clueless!) The cubs climbed nearly a thousand feet up the mountain slope, often passing through stands of rhododendron that were so dense we could not force our way through. In such cases, we had to circle around and hope to find tracks where the cubs had emerged from the brush. Meanwhile, we were wading through snow that was thigh-deep. This went on for a few hours until we were so tired we had to give up and let the cubs live or die on their own. By the time we staggered back downhill to the den site where our colleagues waited, both cubs had long since found their own way back and were again curled up with their mother inside her den.

Fortunately, violent defense by a denned bear is rare with black bears, even mothers with cubs. For example, when a sow black bear with tiny cubs was disturbed in her tree-den as a Vermont logger cut it down, she made no attempt to chastise the intruder.

The same isn't necessarily true with grizzly bears. There have been a number of cases in Scandinavia and North America where someone was attacked near a grizzly/brown bear den. One attack occurred in 1998 when a seismic crew was working twenty miles from my home on Alaska's Kenai Peninsula. Unaware that they were near a grizzly den, the crew walked past it in single file. The frightened bear waited until the last man passed before leaping out and killing him. From a human perspective, once the crew was passed, the danger to the bear was over. But from the bear's standpoint, perhaps it was keyed up to attack but dared not do so until there was only one opponent in sight, with his back to the bear.

The pioneer grizzly bear biologists, John and Frank Craighead, tracked many a grizzly to its den, first by following tracks in the snow; then in later years using radio telemetry. The few times they peeked inside a grizzly den, the bear was awake enough that they dared not try to tranquilize it with a jab stick or capture gun, much less enter the den. One of the few people to safely enter occupied grizzly/brown bear dens was the famous Russian naturalist Vitaly Nikolayenko. Perhaps Nikolayenko got away with this because he was working with brown bears on the Kamchatka Peninsula of Siberia. Those animals, like Alaska's salmon-grizzlies, are far more tolerant of a human intrusion than are salmon-scarce grizzlies far from the coast in North America. Also, Vitaly did this only with a few individual bears that he knew trusted him thoroughly.

Despite the lesser ferocity of black bears, each time you crawl into one of their dens, you can only guess the outcome. Will the bear react typically? Or will this be the one in a thousand bears that attacks? Some black bears just cower at the back of their den; others panic and try to escape; a few threaten violently. But rarely if ever has a black bear injured someone as it tried to escape. Dens usually have just one exit. So the bear has only a few choices: stay put, or go over, under, around, or through the intruder.

My first, and very nearly my last, den visit occurred in Great Smokey Mountains National Park. One chill winter afternoon in 1980, we drove to Cades Cove – and old homestead farm – at the southwestern corner of the Park. Hiking into the mountains, we tracked down a middle-age female black bear by homing in on her transmission. We wanted to learn whether she had produced cubs, and if so, how many, how large, and how healthy. We flipped a coin to see who would crawl into her den. I "won."

5.5: Bear den in the ground (courtesy North American Bear Center).

5.6: Biologist crawling into bear den (courtesy Wisconsin Dept. of Wildlife.

After so much hiking, my cheeks had been hot, even while the tip of my nose had nearly frozen in the subzero weather, and ice-cold sweat dripped down my back. Now, however, as I prepared to enter the den, my blood began to burn. Adrenaline was like high-octane jet fuel. My heart raced, my palms grew slick, and I had to struggle to keep from hyperventilating.

Eager, reluctant, determined, scared, and curious. I started in, using both hands to pull myself forward while holding a small flashlight in my teeth to light the way. About three feet in, the den turned a hairpin corner. To get around the corner, I needed more force than my arms could provide. As my feet thrashed around, trying to find traction on the dirt, my partners thought I was in trouble and dragged me out. I explained and crawled back inside. I rolled onto my right side to bend around the corner. This time, one of the guys used his feet to push against mine, helping me around the corner.

I peered around, trying to spot the bear. Nothing. My beam of light disappeared into stygian darkness. For all I knew, the den might extend back a few body lengths, around another curve or two. I inched forward, gradually bending around the corner until my body was bent in a V-shape with the corner at my waist. I could go no farther.

While lying there, wondering how far ahead the bear was and what to do, I noticed dust particles catching the light, drifting downwards from the ceiling of the den, starting a foot or so in front of my face. Then, ever so slowly, the particles rose a few inches, sank, and rose again. Only as my eyes adjusted to the gloom could I see what lay right before my nose. That dust wasn't hanging in the air ... but resting on the fur of a bear.

A wave of terror swept through me, then faded. I got hold of myself. The bear's breathing was slow and regular. She seemed deep in torpor. Gradually, inch-by-inch, I pulled the syringe of tranquilizer from my shirt, removed the needle-cap, tilted the syringe skywards and squeezed to remove air.

Ignoring the thundering pulse of blood in my ears, striving for courage, I eased the needle up to her rump and shoved – half expecting her to wake up with a roar and tear my head off.

She moved not a muscle. Her breathing seemed to speed up slightly, but I couldn't be sure. Still holding the flashlight between my teeth, I tilted my jaw in various directions to move its beam around to explore the confines of the den, hoping to spot cubs.

Suddenly, my heart spasmed. Looking directly into my eyes, were her eyes. I quit breathing, too frightened to inhale or exhale. The flashlight was still in my mouth. Thrusting my chin forward tipped the flashlight upwards, moving the light off her. Her black pebbly nose was still visible, just inches from my own. She could have licked my face without moving her head.

5.7: Nose to nose. When I entered the bear's den, her head was tucked under, behind her arms out of sight. But when I shoved a hypodermic needle into her rump, her head lifted and she looked right at me. Her nose was so close to my own that she could have licked my face without moving her head – or bitten my face off, had she been so inclined. The sight which greeted me then was similar to this image from the North American Bear Center (Artistic recreation).

Were there two adults in the cave – one with its rump in my face, the other with its nose by mine? No, just a single bear, curled up, nose resting beside her tail.

I dared not make the slightest sound, much less move my upper body. But my legs were kicking frantically to signal my partners to yank me out. They hauled me away but could move me only a few inches. Instead of pulling me out, they just jammed my waist tighter against the hairpin bend in the tunnel.

Even a person or dog or cat could panic at waking up to find itself eyeball to eyeball with a potentially dangerous stranger. Why would a bear be any different?

No more than a few minutes passed, I'm sure, as I waited for the bear to kill me. But for an eternity, she just watched. Finally, her eyelids slowly closed again, as the lethargy of hibernation and the drug took effect.

I shall never know why I survived meeting that sow eyeball to eyeball in her den. Was it solely because she was drowsy from hibernation and perhaps beginning to be sedated by the tranquilizer? Or was she too afraid to attack, or confused and thinking that it was all a bad dream? On the other hand, perhaps she simply preferred avoiding violence.

Once she was fully sedated, we pulled her out of the den and laid her on an insulated blanket. Every ten minutes or so one of us dripped Murine into her eyes to keep them moist and clean. We measured her body dimensions and estimated her fat supply – her bank account of energy essential for surviving until spring when food would again be abundant. The first time she had been captured, several months earlier, a premolar tooth had been removed – which was vestigial and so tiny that removing it inflicted negligible trauma on the bear. This tooth had been sliced open and its rings – like those of a tree – were counted so that we could determine her age. All of these data on age, body size, physiology, and radio locations were necessary for learning how bears differ in the sizes of their home ranges, feeding patterns, and other behaviors critical to their survival in a human-modified landscape. We also replaced her radio-transmitting collar with one that had new batteries which should last at least another year.

I could not help but wonder what it would be like to get to know a wild bear family so well, to be on such good terms with a mother, that she would allow me to share, for some brief while, the hidden world of her birthing chamber. So far, it is only with captive bears that I'd been able to spend the magic weeks before and after the birth of their cubs, as recalled in this excerpt from my previous memoir *Beauty Within the Beast*.

> *I have observed the birth of two bear litters. In the eye of my mind, I can still see the steam rising from the hindquarters of the female I called Soocie as amniotic fluid burst free from her womb and flooded out onto the floor of her den. I recall the gentle plopping sound made by each of the three cubs as they slid out of her body onto the cushion of her lower hind leg, and the slurping of her tongue as she gently removed the amniotic sac and licked them dry. Even now, I seem to hear the first mewing bawls of her neonates, surprisingly loud for such tiny animals, and then the lusty sounds of suckling and the gentle rattle of their purrs.*
>
> *The youngest cubs I have ever held were but hours old, and about the same size as newborn Husky pups – giving no hint of how large they would grow. I felt the cub's warm breath on my lips, their downy soft fur on my cheek and the coolness of their noses against my own. My hands vibrated with their purrs as they sucked on my fingers, vainly seeking milk that I was not equipped to provide.*
>
> *I have looked upon the eyes of cubs before their eyes have seen the world, when their lids were sealed shut, blinding them for their first weeks after birth. When those eyes opened, in the dimness of their natal den, where the only light was snow-filtered translucence, I saw their obsidian pupils afloat in irises like sky blue pools that would one day turn into amber suns, alight with the intelligence and curiosity that make bears among the most intriguing creatures on earth.*

The bear which I called Soocie had originally been named Kit. She and her sister Kate were orphans which had been raised by my mentor Professor Gordon Burghardt at the University of Tennessee. Their first year was spent in his home. When they outgrew that living arrangement, Gordon obtained permission from the Park Service to build a bear-proof enclosure for the cubs on the outskirts of Great Smokey Mountains National Park. Gordon and his grad students continued to study behavior – especially aggression and communication – by these bears for a few years thereafter. But once the bears reached adulthood, their efforts to escape, and efforts by "wild" bears to enter, convinced Gordon of the need for a more secure and permanent home. They were transferred to the Knoxville Zoo, which is where I studied their birthing behavior.

5.8: Den-cam image of "Lily" and her cub, at roughly one month old. Footage can be seen on Youtube and at www.bearstudy.org (Courtesy Wildlife Research Institute).

The Knoxville Zoo had two bear dens, both of which had bare concrete walls and floors, and which opened onto a concrete courtyard exposed to the winter cold and snow. Indoors, the back of Kate's cage was also walled with concrete, except for a metal door. This eliminated any opportunity for me to interact with Kate, although the door's one-foot square window did allow me to watch her preparations for giving birth.

Kit's den, by contrast, was completely open on the back, but interspersed with vertical bars. The bars were spaced widely enough that she and I could both stick an arm through. Although she seemed friendly enough, one of the keepers had lost a finger by sticking it through the window of another bear's cage, whereupon the bear snacked on "finger food." I wasn't about to risk my own finger, hand, or arm.

5.9: In the bad old days up through the 1970's, bears were still kept in concrete compounds which were so barren that they caused severe neurosis if not psychosis. Replacing poured concrete with shotcrete (gunite) carved to simulate rock walls increased aesthetics for humans, but did nothing for bears. However, through the efforts of behavioral biologists like Hal Markotwitz and Else Poulsen (author of *Smiling Bears*) great strides have been made in making bear compounds much more realistic and psychologically healthy for bears.

When Kit was near, I let her do all of the reaching through the bars. She kept trying to grip one of my hands with one of hers, using both her fingers and claws. To be safe, I never let her get a good grip on me. But I did stroke the back of her hand and arm, which she seemed to enjoy. And I provided her with peanuts and raisins, which she enjoyed even more. Had I given all the treats to her all at once, they would have been gone in seconds. Instead, I doled them out a few at a time. They were beyond reach of her long prehensile tongue. So she picked them up one by one, using two claws like chopsticks. This was my first hint that a bear's manual dexterity is far greater than that of a dog or cat –i.e., of a canid or felid. Manual dexterity is closely linked with "intelligence" across a wide variety of animals, from octopi and other cephalopods to carnivores and primates. Increasing dexterity requires more information processing by the brain, which drives brain evolution; reciprocally, greater intelligence allows animals to use their appendages in more ways. This also spurs the development of sensory abilities to precisely control body movements. Dexterity will be addressed much more fully in another book, tentatively called *Reflections on Bears & Apes.*

5.10: Historic photo of a panhandling black bear being fed from the window of a car – a situation which occasionally resulted in someone being swatted or bitten if the bear became frustrated from being fed too little, too slowly (National Park Service Archives).

To my surprise, Kit quickly learned that my feeding her treats only slowly was a game and that all the treats would be forthcoming if she was patient or if she demanded them. Whereas she initially became bored and frustrated, she soon began extending the game until I was the one getting bored. I had lots of other activities to keep me occupied; she didn't. My feeding her this way was critically different from when people stop their car along a roadside to feed a bear. They often dole out food just a bit at a time, while holding more food where it is visible to the bear – which the bear might interpret as being teased. Frustration turns into anger and the bear sometimes bites or claws the hands that fed it too slowly.

5.11: Horace Albright, Yellowstone NP Superintendent 1919 (National Park Service Archives).

Near the end of January, several days before Kit and Kate were expected to give birth, each was given a bale of straw. Each bear dug into her pile, as though hunting through it for food or something else.

Each bear would pile the straw back together into some semblance of a nest, then pull it apart again. This was repeated countless times. I suspected that each was trying to build a nest like it would have made in the wild, but the straw wasn't quite suitable material. When bears did this in the Calgary Zoo, bear keeper Elsie Poulsen interpreted this as fluffing up the straw to make a more comfortable bed.

Concrete rooms are a poor substitute for natural dens. The den dug by a mother bear in the wild begins with a tunnel just big enough for her to fit through; then it is enlarged into a small room with enough space for her to move around, but little more. Each of these zoo dens, by contrast, was at least ten times too large to provide the coziness a bear seeks. The den walls were hard cold concrete, not insulating soft earth that would warm up. In fact, the inside of each den was as cold as the outdoors where temperatures dropped below zero. By contrast, even when outdoor temperatures fall far below zero, the inside of a wild bear's den may not be much below freezing. Snow and earth are good insulators and some heat leaks from the bear's body even when its body temperature has fallen to a low of around 90 degrees F, compared to its active temperature of around 101 degrees. Captive polar bears don't succeed in rearing cubs unless their den is much warmer than what Kit and Kate suffered through in the Knoxville Zoo.

During the weeks leading up to and encompassing birthing by Kit and Kate, I lived in conditions that were almost as harsh, in what might be called a third den beside theirs. It was another concrete room but without access to the outdoors. A small electric heater provided just enough heat to keep my hands from going numb. I slept on a foam mattress and sleeping bag on the icy floor, and cooked meals on a hotplate. An overturned cardboard box served as my desk where I studied for my college courses.

Eventually, I had the joy of watching both sisters give birth, and hearing the first cries and purring of their cubs. Had luck been with me, I would have continued living there for the following months, documenting the development of their cubs. But a few days after the birthings, maintenance work was conducted in the passageway behind the bear cages. The clanging and banging upset Kate so much that she started trying to escape, carrying each cub by its head as she sought a more secure location. But escape was impossible and the cubs did not survive. Kit was also upset. Rather than risk her also losing cubs, everyone avoided her vicinity.

The loss of Kate's cubs was a needless tragedy, created because maintenance personnel were focused on following a pre-ordained work schedule that didn't take into account how the animals would be affected. This was just one more symptom of the difficulties faced when animals are forced to coexist with humans who see them as curiosities, nuisances, vermin, resources, or just non-entities whose needs and preferences are irrelevant. Small wonder that so many "animal lovers" lobby for "animal rights." Although many animal rights proposals are far too extreme to be practical, surely many animals warrant a lot more protection and consideration than is typical even in the 21st century.

My own concern with animal rights began when I mentored orphaned cubs until they could fend for themselves in the Alaska wilderness – as recounted in my first memoir *Beauty Within the Beast*. I was alternately discouraged and infuriated that I had no way to protect them from sport hunters. I had no right to keep on enjoying them alive, whereas anyone with a valid hunting license had a right to kill any or all of them. The cubs had no right to their own lives. Like-wise, even bears and other animals which are protected within national parks usually lose that protection as soon as they set foot outside the park – to say nothing of when a poacher sneaks into the park.

This blasé attitude toward killing any bear that anyone fancies is fostered by the continuing myth that any bear that doesn't flee from people, or that dares threaten someone (if only out of fear), is so dangerous that it needs to be shot. Each of my books recounts additional experiences that evidence the willingness of most bears to live and let live, and that bears that trust and respect people are usually the least dangerous to us.

Experiences during my early studies on grizzly bears are told in

Nearly Breakfast for a Grizzly Bear: Adventures and Observations at Katmai's Brooks River. Since then, I have spent countless hours observing mother grizzly bears and their cubs in more remote areas of Katmai and other regions of Alaska.

Over the course of nearly 20,000 close encounters, I have never been harmed by a bear, and have rarely been in serious danger. That's partly because most bears just prefer to live and let live. But, that said, I am constantly prepared in case I meet a rare bear that isn't so tolerant. Defensive bear viewing is a bit like defensive driving. If you have good brakes, tires with deep tread, and all other systems in top condition, you can drive with confidence, as well as with caution. While driving, I also enjoy the view and constantly look around for interesting sightings. I do the same thing around bears, always hoping for those one-in-a-hundred encounters when they reveal some new, previously unexpected aspect of their nature, perhaps including a capacity and willingness to find friendship with a human.

Tips on how to remain prepared for close encounters are provided in Chapter 1. For more thorough advice, please read the *Alaska Magnum Bear Safety Manual* for basic techniques, and *When Bears Whisper, Do You Listen?* for advanced techniques.

Steve Stringham, Soldotna, Alaska. 2024.

Multimedia for Chapter 5.

RENEWAL

In part because bears can be so dangerous,
they force you to pay attention.
The awe of being in their presence
strips away the chaos of thoughts and distractions
that normally dominate your consciousness.
They focus your attention on the moment.
They flood your blood
with adrenaline and endorphins.
They introduce you to terror, awe,
amazement, and ecstasy.
They connect you to the deepest pulses of life.
This is their gift.
The power to take your life,
or to renew it;
to re-create who you are,
if only for a moment,
and perhaps for a lifetime.

ABOUT THE AUTHOR

Stephen Stringham was born in Colorado, spending his early years at his father's gold mine on Sugarloaf Mountain, west of Boulder, back in the days when the area had more mountain lions than people. At age twelve, he moved with his family to central California, where he soon discovered a fortune in gold whose value at modern prices would be roughly $10 million.

After earning his BSc degree in Biological Oceanography and Marine Ecology, he went on to earn his MSc and Ph.D. degrees studying the behavioral and population ecology of Alaskan moose, European elk (red deer), European mountain goats (chamois), roe deer, and bears. From that time to the present, his research has focused on mother-offspring relations, communication, aggression, roles of adult males, and predator-prey relations.

He later founded WildWatch, an educational services company that engages in basic and applied research, as well as consulting on wildlife issues, and producing educational materials (mainly books and videos) related to wildlife ecology and behavior. He occasionally teaches university courses and tutors K-12 students in math and science.

Along with his wife and soul mate Jacqueline, he has lived and worked in several Native American communities in Montana and Alaska. They are deeply interested in Indigenous Science. All of his activities promote bear conservation – for which he raises funding through writing and selling videos and books, including this one as well as guiding bear viewers and serving as an expert witness in court cases.

Further information about Dr. Stringham is available on his website www.GoBearViewing.com and at his Facebook site Bear Viewing Association. Many of his scientific journal articles and reports can be read on that site. His books can also be previewed there by clicking on the "Books & Videos" tab at the top right of the home page. Information on his courses and consulting is also provided there.

If you would like to join Dr. Stringham in the field to watch bears and learn about them, contact him at GoBearViewing@hotmail.com.

AFTERWORD

Go to hangaripublishing.com to learn more about the Authors and stay up to date with their newest releases.